REDUCED SHAKESPEARE

The Complete Reader's Guide
for the Attention-Impaired
[abridged]

by Reed Martin & Austin Tichenor
of the Reduced Shakespeare Company

New York

Book design and Ars Graphica by Dean Motter
Edited by Howard Zimmerman
Vetted by Dr. Peter Holland, McMeel Family Professor of Shakespeare Studies, University of Notre Dame

Martin, Reed.
    Reduced Shakespeare: The Complete Reader's Guide for the
    Attention-Impaired (abridged)/Reed Martin, Austin Tichenor.--1st ed.
        p. cm.
    Includes bibliographic references and index.
    ISBN 1-4013-0220-3
    1. Shakespeare, William, 1564–1616—Handbooks, manuals, etc. 2.
    Shakespeare, William, 1564–1616—Outlines, syllabi, etc. 3. Shakespeare,
    William, 1564–1616—Humor. I. Tichenor, Austin II. Reduced Shakespeare
    Company III. Title

    PR2895.M375 2006
    822.3'3—dc22

FIRST EDITION

10 9 8 7 6 5 4 3 2 1

This book is dedicated to
the men and women
(and men who play women)
of the
REDUCED SHAKESPEARE COMPANY

Since brevity is the soul of wit,
we shall be brief :

Thanks

TABLE OF CONTENTS

re·duced

(ri-'düst, ri-'dyüst)

Middle English; from the Latin *reducere*: to lead

1 a : drawn together, converged : CONSOLIDATED

b: decreased volume and concentrated flavor : BOILED

c : narrowed down, shortened : ABRIDGED

2 : broken down (as by crushing or grinding) : PULVERIZED

3 : converted : see also CONQUERED

INTRODUCTION

"Who is it that can tell me who I am?"
King Lear, Act I, Scene 4

hy have we written this book? Let us count the ways:

1) Because we're fed up. There are simply too many Shakespeare books out there, most of which are an utter waste of paper and readers' time, and the issue needs to be addressed. Where can any reader—from the mildly curious dabbler to the most rabid Shakespeare geek—learn everything he or she needs to know about the greatest dramatic poet the world has ever known? Somebody, somewhere needs to boil down all the pertinent information into one brilliantly concise, intellectually cogent, and entertainingly readable volume. Until somebody does that, we've written this.

2) Because the plays are too long. Who has the time to sit through four-hour productions? Why doesn't somebody cut out all the minor characters and unimportant subplots and get right to the sex and the killing, which is what people really want to see?

3) Because they're complicated. Yes, we know the poetry's amazing and it's cool that this 400-year-old playwright continues to speak to us today—but what language is he speaking?

Fig 1. The first of many depictions of a man who looks like what we think Shakespeare looked like.

WHAT'S A GROUNDLING?

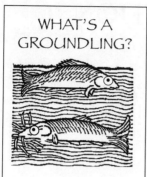

In Shakespeare's time, the common folk who couldn't afford to pay for a seat bought standing-room tickets down near the stage. They were called "groundlings" after a type of fish that lives on the bottom of lakes and streams. The actors on-stage saw the audience staring up at them wide-eyed and open-mouthed (from the *ground*) and were amused by the similarity. The name stuck. Interestingly, rich people who could afford tickets bought seats in the half-ring of seating above. These people were called "ringlings" and were so inspired by the work of Shakespeare they later moved to America and started a circus.

4) Because everybody says he's a genius. Fine. But what does that *mean*? What *kind* of genius? Was he born that way, or did he pick it up somewhere? Was there something in the water? Is there any way that some of it will rub off on us if we write a book about him?

5) Because we want to know who William Shakespeare *was*. What do we know about him? What do we only *think* we know about him? What's the best way to begin to explore the man, the myth, the mystery, the master, and his masterpieces?[1]

These and many other questions will be asked and answered throughout the course of our exploration. This one book contains everything you'll ever need to know about the Bard of Avon. Burn the other ones—this book is all you need.

For those of you completely uninitiated into the cult of Shakespeare, we just want to say two things: One, congratulations; two, don't worry, our approach will be very simple. You see, over the centuries Shakespeare's been put up on a pedestal. In his time his plays were popular culture: Everyone loved them, from royalty to the groundlings. But now his work is

---

[1] And is alliteration really the best way to start?

considered "high" culture, and the sad fact is that today, Shakespeare intimidates people.

In this book we fight back. We kick the pedestal out from under Shakespeare and make him accessible once again to the grubby, semiliterate, easily distracted masses. Um, present company excepted, of course.

So what do you need to know about Shakespeare? Just this: The entire Shakespeare industry consists of people simply guessing about who Shakespeare was and what he wrote. For centuries, generations of literary scholars, historians, researchers, psychologists, scientists—realists and fantasists of every possible persuasion—have delved into the life and works—and mystery—of William Shakespeare. Not knowing much about Shakespeare's life hasn't stopped everyone from cashing in, filling in the blanks with scholarly supposition when they can, and simply making it up ("Shakespeare *must have* known/done/learned/lived... ") when they can't.

It's a shocking record, and we're proud to be part of it.

This book exists to explode the Shakespeare myth once and for all; to lay out the facts and expose the lies; to make Shakespeare fun and easy to understand, and accessible; and to spell out everything a moderately intelligent person needs to know about the Bard of Stratford.[2]

By the time you finish this single tome you will know everything

---

[2] And to make a few bucks.

you need to know about the life and work of William Q. Shakespeare:

- his life in Stratford
- his life in London
- his marriage
- his family
- his writing
- the source(s) of his genius
- his shabby real-estate deals
- his endless forays into rehab
- his legendary and much-publicized affairs with supermodels.

Ultimately you will understand that Shakespeare is revered above all other writers not because of the kind of man he was but because of his works. And you, too, will be awed by the remarkable texts that comprise:

- Shakespeare's plays
- Shakespeare's poetry
- Shakespeare's movies.

In this one invaluable volume, we'll reveal the facts of Shakespeare's life and uncover the fiction, getting closer to the core of the poet's

genius than any scholar has ever attempted. Come, rub elbows with us as we stand shoulder to shoulder alongside this literary giant, and let the dandruff of his greatness fall upon you.

Read, lather, rinse, repeat.

And enjoy.

Shakespeare Quiz

Do you know the answers to these twenty questions?
You still won't after reading this book, which is why the answers
are listed on pages 221–223.

1. What is believed to be the first play that Shakespeare wrote?
2. What is believed to be the last play he wrote?
3. Which two books did Shakespeare use as general references for his history plays?
4. Name the four major poems attributed to Shakespeare, other than the sonnets.
5. Which two monarchs ruled England during Shakespeare's lifetime?
6. What is the First Folio? Name the two people most responsible for its publication.
7. What is a Quarto?
8. Name four London theaters in which Shakespeare's plays may have been first performed.
9. How many plays are generally attributed to Shakespeare?
10. How many sonnets are attributed to him?
11. How many children did Shakespeare have?
12. How many brothers and sisters did Shakespeare have?
13. What were the names of Shakespeare's parents?
14. What was the name of Shakespeare's dog?
15. What was the name of his wife?
16. Where was Shakespeare both born and buried?
17. Which two actors were *not* members of Shakespeare's acting company: Richard Burbage, Henry Condell, John Hemminges, Harry Dean Stanton, William Kemp, Robert Armin, Thomas Pope, Augustine Phillips, or Jerry Mathers?
18. Who is believed to be the "Dark Lady" of the Sonnets?
19. What type of verse did Shakespeare use most commonly in his plays?
20. Which of Shakespeare's plays was likely the most popular during his lifetime?

WILLIAM SHAKESPEARE'S LIFE STORY

Part One
The Disclaimer

"O! for a muse of fire,
that would ascend the brightest heaven of invention."
Henry V, Prologue

it down, children,
and we'll tell you the story of
William Shakespeare.

But first, a disclaimer. Truth-in-biography laws require us to reveal that all Shakespeare biographies must from now on be displayed in the Fiction section of bookstores and libraries.

If you found this book in the Theater or Biography sections (or, as is more likely, on the remainder table), you have been the victim of a fraud. There just aren't enough facts known about Shakespeare's actual life to tell you absolutely for certain what he did or when he did it. Shakespeare's life is one of the most exhaustively researched in the history of literature, and

Fig. 2. The Droeshout Engraving, considered by scholars to be the definitive guess as to what the dude looked like.

Personal Diary of

William Shakespeare

Things to Do Today

in this Year of Our Lord 1601

1. Begin tribute to Her Majesty
(working title: The Regina Monologues)
2. Dump mistress
   - get a Blond Lady of the Sonnets
3. Finish Richard IV—The Revenge
4. More glove imagery!
5. Inform Lord Meineke I'll be recompensed withal; I
      needs must have a woolen scarf and shan't pay a
      lot for this muffler.
6. Take out garbage (including Timon of Athens)
7. Get plague shots
8. Ignore wife and kids in Stratford more
9. Toupee, or not Toupee?
10. Burn all personal papers. Posterity can bite me.

Fig. 3. Written evidence of Shakespeare's life and work *not* found by scholars and historians despite centuries of looking.

new details about the world and people of Shakespeare's time are uncovered every year. Yet scholars *still* haven't uncovered (for instance) Shakespeare's workbooks, rough drafts, love letters to his wife and/or mistress (unless you count the sonnets, which for the purposes of this disclaimer, we don't), airplane reservations in his name, diaries (see figure 3), or a third-grade class picture with Shakespeare's nine-year-old bald head gleaming like an Elizabethan dodge ball.

We know some things, which we'll identify when we come to them, but by and large the field of Shakespearean biography is one of conjecture and mighty leaps of imagination. Because so few historical facts exist, biographers must drink deeply of Shakespeare's "muse of fire" and rise to the "brightest heaven of invention." In other words, they make stuff up. Otherwise, they got no book.

Scholars often talk about Shakespeare's "lost years," but really, in terms of the documentary evidence, they're *all* lost years. When we call the events of Shakespeare's life a story we're not just being cute (because, among other things, one glance at the back cover will tell you that's impossible). We call it a story because that's what it is: information, speculation, and conjecture dancing a delightful *ménage à trois* with earrings in one ear and bandannas in back pockets, signaling a deep commitment to fact, but also a willingness to explore other possibilities.

It's a tale, in fact. And in this case told by idiots.

Now, on with our story.

HISTORICAL TIMELINE

October 23, 4004 BC, 9 AM (GMT) – Big Bang (known sometimes as God) creates universe from two protons (known sometimes as Adam & Eve; check local statutes for what's accepted as fact in your area). Genius of William Shakespeare already anticipated as historical inevitability.

1564 – William Shakespeare is born in Stratford-upon-Avon.

Christopher Marlowe and Galileo also born this year, but not in Stratford. In transportation news, horse-drawn carriage is introduced in England.

1565 – Graphite pencils first manufactured in England.

1566 – Nostradamus dies. He didn't see it coming.

1558 – Elizabeth I assumes the throne.

1559 – Elizabeth helps Scotland free itself of France.

1562 – Milled coins are introduced. 369 years later, the Mills Brothers cut their first record.

1567 – Sir Francis Drake sets sail for the New World. 1569 – Mercator map published, first comprehensive map of the world.

1577 – "The Curtain" opens. It's "a theater," not " The Theater."

1576 – Richard Burbage opens "The Theater" playhouse in London.

1575 – Population of London is 180,000. Population of Paris is 300,000.

1571 – Johann Kepler (German Astronomer) born.

1579 – Sir Francis Drake discovers what is now San Francisco.

1581 – Queen Elizabeth I, in Greenwich, sees Sir Francis Drake's Golden Hind. Rethinks Virgin status.

1584 – Sir Walter Raleigh discovers what is now Virginia and claims it for England. Ivan the Terrible becomes Ivan the Dead.

1585 – June 13, the only recorded date in history when there was absolutely no fighting between Catholics and Protestants, Jews and Arabs, or Republicans and Democrats. Shakespeare and Anne Hathaway, however, had a huge dustup. Shakespeare subsequently moves to London.

1591 – Shakespeare's *Henry VI, Parts 2 & 3* premiere, as does Marlowe's *The Jew of Malta*.

1590 – Ronald Reagan born.

1588 – English navy defeats the Spanish Armada in overtime. Marlowe's *Doctor Faustus* premieres. Thomas Hobbes is born.

1587 – Elizabeth has her Catholic half-sister, Mary Queen of Scots, beheaded. Marlowe's *Tamburlaine* premieres, as does Thomas Kyd's *The Spanish Tragedy*.

1586 – Kabuki theater begins in Japan.

1592 – Shakespeare's *Richard III* and *Comedy of Errors* premiere. Plague kills 15,000 people in London. Theaters close.

1593 – Marlowe killed in tavern fight.

1594 – London theaters reopen. Thomas Kyd is buried 15 August; historians conclude with some certainty that he must have been dead.

1595 –Shakespeare premieres *Romeo and Juliet*, *Richard II*, and *A Midsummer Night's Dream*.

1600 – Telescope invented. Galileo starts pissing off the Pope.

1599 – Oliver Cromwell born. Globe Theater is built in London. *Henry V* and *Julius Caesar* premiere.

1598 – Ben Jonson – *Every Man in His Humour.*

1597 – *Henry IV, Parts 1 & 2.*

1596 – Blackfriars Theater opens in London. Rene Descartes is born. Sir Francis Drake dies. Galileo invents the thermometer. In a painful accident, he also invents the rectal thermometer.

1601 – *Hamlet* and *Twelfth Night* premiere.

1602 – Dutch East India Company founded – first modern public company.

1603 – Elizabeth I dies. James VI of Scotland becomes King James I of England, uniting the countries under the new name Great Britain. Ireland is strangely silent. Many scholars believe James I was gay. Not that there's anything wrong with that.

1605 – Guy Fawkes attempts to blow up Parliament. Cervantes publishes *Don Quixote*. *King Lear* opens.

1606 – *Macbeth* premieres, as does Ben Jonson's *Volpone*. Rembrandt is born.

1610 – Ben Jonson's *The Alchemist*. Shakespeare's *The Winter's Tale*. Dutch East India Company introduces the term "share." In an amazing coincidence, Henry Hudson discovers Hudson Bay. Pilgrims land at Plymouth Rock, Massachusetts, and immediately elect a Kennedy.

1609 – For the first time ever, tea is shipped from China to Europe by the Dutch East India Company.

1608 – Checks are first used for monetary transactions.

1607 – Jamestown colony is founded, first English settlement in North America.

1611 – Shakespeare's *The Tempest*. King James allows Jamestown colonists to grow hemp. 357 years later, *High Times* is first published.

1612 – John Webster's *The White Devil*. Last recorded burning of heretics in England. Speaking of smoking, tobacco is first planted in Virginia.

1613 – Shakespeare's *Henry VIII*. Globe Theater in London is destroyed by fire during performance of *Henry V*.

1614 – John Webster's *Duchess of Malfi*. Pocahontas marries John Rolfe.

1615 – Galileo first faces the Inquisition.

1981 – Reduced Shakespeare Company founded.

1964 – Keanu Reeves born.

1623 – First Folio published.

1618 – Sir Walter Raleigh executed, muddy cloak and all.

1616 – William Shakespeare dies. Miguel de Cervantes also dies, quite possibly on the exact same day but in an "apparently unrelated" incident. First ship sails around Cape Horn. Galileo is prohibited from further scientific work.

WILLIAM SHAKESPEARE'S LIFE STORY

Part Two

The Early Years

"One man in his time plays many parts…"
As You Like It, Act II, Scene 7

illiam Shakespeare was the third of eight children, born to John Shakespeare and the former Mary Arden on or about April 23, 1564.[3]

He was born in Stratford-upon-Avon,[4] a small town 100 miles northwest of London. Hard as it is to believe, young William was born into a world in which the name Shakespeare was not yet synonymous with "genius poet." The name *Shakespeare*, in fact, meant nothing at all.

His mother's maiden name, on the other hand, was quite well known and meaningful: The Arden name went back at least 500 years to its appearance in the Domesday Book, the medieval census conducted by William the Conqueror in 1086 to ensure that everybody was paying enough tax, and the Forest of Arden itself

Fig. 4. This ruffled dandy thinks he's all that and a bag of chips. Is he Shakespeare? Scholars are divided.

---

[3] We say "on or about" because the only evidence we have of Shakespeare's birth is the record of his baptism on April 26, which generally happened three days after the baby was born.

[4] We say "Stratford-upon-Avon" because that's its name.

Fig. 5. Bearbaiting in progress

(named for Mary's illustrious ancestors) was (and still is) within spitting distance of Stratford.

William's father, John Shakespeare, was many things: A glove-maker, a leather dresser (which was a man who prepared leather for making gloves and belts, not one of the Village People), a real-estate investor, a commodities trader (dealing largely with wool and grain, sometimes on the black market), and a local politician who rose from chamberlain to burgess to alderman until ultimately sitting on the town council as high bailiff, in effect becoming the mayor of Stratford. A dilettante, perhaps? A dabbler, you say? No, John Shakespeare was a *survivor*: a man who knew that expertise in only one field wouldn't be enough to support his family. (It's an example William would follow.[5]) The guy skated close to the edge: he ultimately went bankrupt, lost most of his assets, stopped showing his face at town council meetings, and in a final indignity applied for a family coat of arms and was denied. (These examples William managed to avoid repeating.)

---

[5] For a more detailed examination of John Shakespeare's political life, rent *Elizabethan Survivor: Stratford Town Council*. John was voted off in an early round.

There's no evidence Shakespeare attended school, but as Norrie Epstein points out in *The Friendly Shakespeare*, there's no evidence that he didn't, either. That he must have attended elementary school in Stratford is one of those leaps (like the previous ones about Shakespeare's following his father's examples and avoiding his mistakes) it seems fairly safe to make. He was also probably very good at history since there was so much less of it to learn then.

Whether he saw any theater as a child, however, is another matter. Troupes of traveling players went from town to town and had to audition for the local leaders, so some scholars insist that, because of John Shakespeare's high office, Shakespeare must have watched performances of plays, enrapt, at his father's knee. Maybe. This assumes his father had a knee. There's no evidence that he did have knees but there's no evidence that he didn't, either. Certainly Shakespeare would have been aware of performing: Elizabethan England was a nonstop cavalcade of religious festivals and seasonal celebrations, filled with the kind of dancing and rustic jollity that always looks so forced when you see it at Renaissance Faires today. Then, as now, the main appeal of

SHAKESPEARE'S FAVORITE SPORTS

Shakespeare probably enjoyed the sports of his day (bearbaiting, cock fighting) as much as the next genius, but as a Renaissance Man he also enjoyed a wide range of more eclectic competitions. Here are a few of them:

The Iambic Pentathlon

Pin the Blame
on the Plantagenets

Actors-in-Drag Racing

Arena Football

Synchronized
Swimming

The War of
the Rose Bowl

Twelfth Night Football
Hangman

Timon of Athens
Olympics

Nascart Racing

Hop Scots

Serfing

WILLIAM SHAKESPEARE: FAILED GLOVER

Shakespeare's fledgling poetic abilities crop up in another account, possibly a suburban myth. Legend has it that the gloves young Shakespeare made never perfectly matched the hands of his clients. Numerous patrons complained, in their English slang, about Shakespeare's uncomfortable "bloody gloves." Eventually, he left the trade altogether, reputedly telling his father (in a perfect ten-syllable iambic line), "My gloves they do not fit, so I must quit." The glove business's loss was literature's gain.

these pastoral events was beer and cleavage.

Shakespeare probably did not attend formal university. England had only two universities in Shakespeare's day—Oxford and Cambridge—and it's very unlikely that anyone from Shakespeare's class would have gone.[6] Besides, who had the time? The evidence clearly shows he was enrolled in the University of Life. Shakespeare became a father and married Anne Hathaway while still in his teens, and in almost that order. Six months after the wedding, Anne gave birth to Susanna Shakespeare. Scientists are still split about what to make of this phenomenon: either human gestation in the sixteenth-century was much faster than it is today, or apparently it was possible back then for a woman to get pregnant without actually being married.

So how did Shakespeare support his young family? Tradition has often assumed that he apprenticed in his father's glove-making trade, as his plays are filled with references to the tools and details of that life. For instance, Mistress Quickly in *The Merry Wives of Windsor* refers to "a glover's paring knife," and Mercutio jokes about Romeo's "wit of cheveril" (a very soft and flexible kid-skin).

---

[6] "Class" in this case refers to Shakespeare's social status, not the crazy wacked-out dudes from Stratford High Class of 1582.

There are also suggestions that Shakespeare might have turned his prodigious talent to the greeting card trade: "The gift is small, the will is all / Alexander Aspinall" accompanied a pair of gloves that Master Aspinall presented to a woman he was courting, and which presumably he bought at John Shakespeare's shop. Could shop-clerk William have scribbled this Elizabethan Hallmark moment, which included the self-promoting pun on his own name?

Recent speculation also suggests that Shakespeare spent time as a tutor and/or schoolmaster, possibly in Lancashire, based on hints found in the records of various Catholic teachers (several of whom had ties to Stratford), as well as a man named Alexander Hoghton, who decreed in his will that his brother should "keep and maintain players," as well as "be friendly unto . . . William Shakeshafte." People like this idea of Shakespeare teaching and joining a troupe of actors because it explains how he might have stumbled into the theater.

There's only one problem: as even semiliterates like ourselves can tell, *Shakeshafte* isn't the same as *Shakespeare*; it doesn't even sound the same. This points up something which is embarrassing for the seasoned Shakespeare biographer to admit but really must be said: Much of the "evidence" collected over the centuries consists of different names found in ancient handwritten records that are assumed to refer to Shakespeare but are spelled variously as Shakesper, Shakspere, Shakeshafte, Shagsbere, Shaxpere, Shaquille, Shaxpaire, Christopher Marlowe, Shakestuff, Shakeyerbooty, and (for some reason) Keith.[7] There's very little compelling evidence that William Shakspere, the man who was born in Stratford, is the same person as William *Shakespeare*, the world-famous poet and playwright (except for the knowledge that

---

[7] Bert Fields discusses this fully (and calmly) in *Players: The Mysterious Identity of William Shakespeare*. As you might expect from a noted entertainment lawyer, it's a bare-bones, slightly dry but always fascinating, just-the-facts-ma'am approach to the question of Shakespeare's identity, with absolutely none of that annoying "Shakespeare must have done this" kind of conjecture... um, until the very end, when he trips and falls shoulder-deep in it. It's well-reasoned, imaginatively created, and persuasively argued—but it's conjecture nonetheless.

seventeenth-century spelling was as loose as the women who plied their trade around the Globe Theater).

Depending on your medication, all these discrepancies are either a) a major obstacle, or 2) no big deal. It's your call, but next time an orthodox Stratfordian suggests you're ready for the rubber room because you doubt the "evidence," and won-ders how you can question whether Stratford Shakspere isn't Poet Shakespeare, tell him you do so with the same ease that he accepts all those misspellings as simply Elizabethan typos.[8]

There are other critics who doubt Shakespeare's ability to write knowledgeably about, well, everything, because he lacked educa-tion and position. (These are clearly critics who want to deny Shakespeare's genius, which is by definition inexplicable, or else it wouldn't be genius.) But maybe we can better understand the Man from Stratford by discussing the turbulent world in which he lived.

---

[8] The glitches aren't limited to William. His bride is listed in two places as "An-nam Whateley" and "Anne Hathwey." Most people accept that William wasn't "torn between two lovers" (to use the phrase from the hit song of the '70s—the 1570s) that these are only slips of the Elizabethan pen. And to be fair, that's an easy idea to accept. Should we really expect spelling consistency from a society that used lower case f's for s's? Serioufly, their fpelling waf fhitty.

ESSAY QUESTION: *In 1552, John Shakespeare was fined for maintaining a dunghill in the middle of Henley Street. Describe how Shakespeare paid tribute to his father by writing the steaming pile of crap called* Coriolanus.

WILLIAM SHAKESPEARE'S LIFE STORY

Part Three

Reformation & Counter-Reformation

"Men at some time are masters of their fates.
The fault, dear Brutus, is not in our stars
But in ourselves. . ."
Julius Caesar, Act 1, Scene 2

 eah, but the stars help.

Shakespeare's genius is evident by noting the groundbreaking dramaturgy of his plays: their pre-Freudian psychological insights, monumental stagecraft, impeccable showmanship, and dazzling wordplay.

But you could argue (and we will) that he was also a *marketing* genius: a savvy judge of the public mind who knew what subjects would play well before his audiences (and would therefore put more money in his pockets by putting more butts in the seats). He was also a savvy judge of the *royal* mind, knowing what he could say without drawing the condemnation of the censor or execution by the Queen.

But the greatest example of Shakespeare's genius is simply this: his decision to be born in 1564. Sixteenth-century England was a furnace, a crucible, a burning-hot metaphor thing that forged the destinies of all who lived within it. Politics and religion were inextricably intertwined. When King Henry VIII (he of the six wives; fabled in song[9] and in Shakespeare's second-to-last—and

---

[9] Cf: Hermits, Herman's. 1964.

defiantly least—play; see p. 61) began his reign in 1509, he was an ardent Catholic who had actually written a book attacking Martin Luther's Protestant Reformation. Pope Leo X even gave Henry the title "Defender of the Faith," a title English monarchs retain today because it sounds better than "Rejecter of the Faith."

Because oh, how faith can change when you want a divorce and the Pope won't allow it. When his wife proved unable to bear him a son (and without considering the possibility that maybe it was his own fault), Henry VIII found himself in a pickle. As a Catholic he couldn't divorce; as a monarch he needed a male heir. So he started his own church, one that would allow divorce. This seemed a bit more civilized than beheading your wife in order to remarry. Henry had tried that, too. It's a long story.

In establishing the Church of England (with himself as its head) Henry not only renounced the dictates of Rome but also executed any Catholics who objected to it. He brought the Protestant Reformation, brutally, to England.

And when he died, Henry VIII's nine-year-old son, King Edward VI, was not able to stem the tide of religious violence and bloodshed.[10] Nor was Lady Jane Grey, who at age fifteen was appointed Queen pretty much against her will when Edward died (also at age fifteen), but who nonetheless reigned for a glorious and relatively bloodshed-free total of nine days.

Henry VIII's daughter Mary (from his divorced wife Catherine of Aragon, half sister to Edward) had a strong legitimate claim to the throne and not even her unapologetic Catholicism could keep her off it. Once installed as Queen, and eager to restore England to the true faith, Mary opened up a can of Catholic counter-Reformation whup-ass, condemning and executing many prominent Protestants, including the Archbishop of Canterbury. The poor English didn't know what hit them: Apparently, it wasn't safe to be Catholic *or* Protestant.

Fortunately, Henry VIII's *other* legitimate daughter became

---

[10] Yes, Henry had finally managed to plant a boy into his third wife Jane Seymour. Obviously this was long before she starred as TV's *Dr. Quinn, Medicine Woman*.

Queen Elizabeth I when Mary died in 1558. Compared with the Goldilocks excesses of Henry VIII and "Bloody Mary," Queen Elizabeth was *juuust* right. Famously proclaiming that she refused "to make windows into men's souls," and that "there is only one Jesus Christ and all the rest is a dispute over trifles," Elizabeth instituted history's first "Don't ask, don't tell" policy regarding matters of faith. Still, the era wasn't violence-free. The Puritans—those champions of religious freedom that Americans hear so much about—thought the Church of England was still too permissive and tolerant; and Queen Elizabeth was rightly paranoid and (perhaps not so rightly) trigger-happy when it came to rumors of treason and usurpation. But the rampant nationwide civil bloodshed did slow to a dribble.

So when anti-Stratfordians harp on about how it's impossible for Shakespeare to have written so knowledgeably about the turmoil of political court life because he was an uneducated, untitled glove-maker's son, they miss the fact that this drama and intrigue played itself out in every aspect of Shakespeare's everyday life. Shakespeare couldn't escape danger and intrigue: it colored every decision and relationship the man had. You couldn't swing a dead plague-ridden cat without hitting somebody who was deeply conflicted about what he could or could not say or believe. The English monarchy—and thus, the official state religion—had gone from Catholic to Protestant to Catholic to Protestant within the space of twelve years. In this context, and in this time and place in history, you would have had to be a mentally retarded illiterate *not* to have written thirty-nine of the greatest plays in the history of the English-speaking stage.[11]

Think about it: Shakespeare might have been born centuries before there even was such a thing as theater, or before Gutenberg had invented movable type, which allowed Shakespeare's plays to be printed and read by millions of bored high school students. He could have been born just eighty years later, during Cromwell's Reign of Terror when theater was outlawed. He could have been born in America in the 1980s when Republicans started cutting arts funding. But no—Shakespeare knew that the second half of the

---

[11] We say this because it's a sweeping overstatement.

Fig. 6. Shakespeare was far ahead of his time. Here we see the first actor to ever "come out of the closet" in an early production of *Merry Wives of Windsor*.

sixteenth century was the perfect time where he could make the greatest lasting impression. And he was right. Talk about getting in on the ground floor. As we've said, everybody says Shakespeare was a genius but nobody tells you why. This is one of the reasons.[12]

It's probably hard for modern readers to understand just how different things were in the late sixteenth century. Unlike today, people of different religions had no tolerance for each other; back then, believers of one faith thought they were right, everyone else was wrong, and that it was their holy duty to convert everyone else to their own point of view.

Fortunately, now, almost 500 years later, these myopic religious views and extremist sectarianism have completely disappeared.

If, as the evidence suggests, Shakespeare's family members were closeted Catholics in an increasingly Protestant England, it seems equally obvious that Shakespeare himself kept a low profile, religion-wise. And maybe this combination of destiny and achievement is the bedrock of Shakespeare's success. He clearly had a talent for taking the conflict he observed in life and portraying it onstage.

---

[12] Christopher Marlowe was *thisclose* to being a genius: he was also born in 1564, but he died young, killed—suspiciously—in a tavern brawl. Does this sound like genius to you? We didn't think so.

But perhaps his greatest gift, his true genius, was in simply keeping his head down. Perhaps he realized, as Michael Wood puts it in his excellent film *In Search of Shakespeare*, that "great art, great poetry, comes not by choosing one side—but by seeing both."

Fig. 7. Our favorite part of *The New Yorker* magazine is the page where they invite readers to make up their own caption. We invite you to do that here.

ESSAY QUESTION: *In Shakespeare's day, Elizabeth became the Queen because her father had been the King. This is called a "monarchy." America is what's known as a "democracy." That's why, in the early twenty-first century, George W. Bush became the president because his father had also been the president . . . hey, wait a minute! Discuss.*

LONDON THROUGH THE CENTURIES

Shakespeare's London. Note "The Globe" on the Southside of the Thames.

London in 1941 - The Blitz. Note heavy destruction, evidence of Nazi leader Hermann Goering's determination to "bomb England back to the Elizabethan Age."

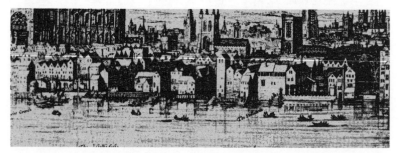

London Today. Note the attention to detail and precision with which England has reimagined itself as Shakespeare Land.

WILLIAM SHAKESPEARE'S LIFE STORY

Part Four

London Calling

"If I can make it there, I'll make it anywhere..."
Troilus and Cressida, Act VI, Scene 12

hh, London... or as the early Romans and 1960s Batman called it, Londinium.

'Twas a paradise on earth, the jewel of sixteenth-century Europe — or, as a responsible opposing viewpoint has it, "a great deal like twentieth-century Calcutta."[13]

Chamber pots were emptied into the streets, usually after a warning cry of "Gardee loo!"—but sometimes before.[14] Rats and raw sewage ran freely through the streets because the greatest scientific minds of the day had concluded in their infinite wisdom that bubonic plague was airborne. (It isn't.)

The heads of traitors were stuck on spikes and displayed for all to see on London Bridge (Shakespeare refers to this in *Richard III*). Sailors from the many vessels tied up at the city's wharves disembarked looking for liquor, action, and whores, all of which were readily available. Pickpockets roamed the streets. The death rate exceeded the birthrate, yet the city's population continued

---

[13] A. L. Beier, *Masterless Men,* p. 84, quoted in Peter Thomson's *Shakespeare's Professional Career,* p. 116. Also quoted here, obviously.
[14] "Gardee loo" is Anglicized French for *Gardez l'eau,* that is "watch out for the water (gardez l'eau)!"

to swell as people poured into London from the country, seeking their fortunes among the fetid teeming multitudes. And, of course, government-sanctioned terrorism allowed Catholics and Protestants to harass and murder one another, depending on who sat on the throne. Good times, people. Good times.

Then, as now, London called to the aspiring writer, "Hey, hot-shot in Nowhere-on-Avon! Wanna try a *real* city on for size?" Shakespeare heard this siren call and like millions of his country-men before and since made his way to the capital city of London, only nobody knows when or how. One persistent legend says Shakespeare was caught poaching deer and had to flee Stratford to escape prosecution. Others speculate that he joined a troupe of traveling players and simply returned with them to their London base. But as we know Shakespeare's wife gave birth to the twins Judith and Hamnet in 1585, and because that's the last record we have of Shakespeare for seven years, it seems safe to conclude that Shakespeare took one look at three mewling puking babies, snapped his fingers as he remembered the theatrical destiny that awaited him, shouted the immortal words "I'm outta here," and split for the city.

Poetic genius? Absolutely. Devoted family man? Not so much.

Whatever the impetus, it's clear that William had a dream.[15] The rewards of small-town glove making, local politics, and hands-on fatherhood were clearly not for him. Something gnawed at his soul, even if it was only the realization that the make-believe world of the theater was something at which he could excel.

Somehow, the record doesn't tell us, Shakespeare hooked up with an acting company. Whether it was in London or out in the country, we have no idea. So let's say it was definitely out in the country.

Clearly, he was a success with whichever company he worked. Young people who join acting companies only *remain* with acting companies by making themselves invaluable through hard work, blazing talent, a willingness to pitch in, or some combination of

---

[15] We say this because it's pure conjecture.

all three.[16] At first, Shakespeare was probably allowed to play small parts in exchange for distributing flyers, hauling props, mending costumes, assisting the prompter, or emptying the actors' piss pots.[17]

Whatever the arrangement, Shakespeare followed his father's example and took on as many jobs as it took.

It's unclear whether Shakespeare was a writer first and actor second, or an actor who became a poet and then (although the word didn't even exist then) a playwright. The evidence suggests it was the latter: At the very least Shakespeare was *perceived* as an actor who dared to dabble in the literary arts.

How do we know this? In 1592, in the first recorded reference to Shakespeare in London, the dying dramatist Robert Greene bitterly referred to Shakespeare as an "upstart crow" who, *"beautified with our* [i.e., writers'] *feathers...supposes he is as well able to bombast out a blank verse as the best of you: and...is in his own conceit the only Shake-scene in the country."* Well! Clearly the "player" Shakespeare was doing something right: He was successful enough to warrant a public dressing down from a prominent (though now largely forgotten) dramatist.

Then as now, acting was a risky way to make a living; making things doubly difficult was that an actor couldn't just hang around waiting for his next gig, or wander itinerantly from troupe

Fig. 8. Upstart crow William Shakespeare on left. Russell Crowe on right.

---

[16] It's also possible that that first acting company let him in because Shakespeare had a van, would work for free, or was sleeping with the artistic director. The historical record is unclear.

[17] In the days before indoor plumbing, disposing of human waste was a major stepping-stone to success and, in rare cases, a knighthood. (See also *Shitpot: The Rise of Sir Walter "Stinky" Raleigh*.)

to troupe. In Elizabethan England unaffiliated actors could be arrested, beaten, and deported as a vagrants.[18] An actor needed a company and a company needed a patron—a wealthy benefactor who could pay the company's expenses and whose glory the company would reflect.[19]

Forget about being a genius for a second. The real art of the theater is making a living at it. Not everybody can do it. But Shakespeare did: he not only squeaked by, he succeeded and flourished; first as an actor, and ultimately as a company owner, shareholder, grain hoarder, real-estate magnate, and country gentleman.

How did he accomplish all this? No one knows. As Philip Henslowe says in the movie *Shakespeare in Love*, "It's a mystery," and like the mysteries concerning the source of Shakespeare's genius, it's one we'll attempt to solve.

Unconventional Wisdom

Recent scholarship has changed much of our thinking about William Shakespeare. Throughout the book we'll highlight several areas in which our understanding of the great poet has deepened and strengthened.

The Conventional Wisdom: As a young man, Shakespeare left Stratford after he was caught poaching in the deer park of a local justice of the peace.

The Reduced Wisdom: Shakespeare left Stratford after he was caught "shaking his spear" in the deer park of a local justice of the peace.

ESSAY QUESTION: *When they're brushing their teeth, our children cry "Gardee loo" when they're about to spit into the sink. Adorable worldly moppets or precocious little shits? Discuss.*

---

[18] The same, alas, is true today.

[19] And whose patronizing attitude and condescension the actors would have to endure.

WILLIAM SHAKESPEARE'S LIFE STORY

Part Five

Glory Days

"I have touched the highest point of all my greatness…"
Henry VIII, Act III, Scene 2

hese were heady days for young Will Shakespeare.

Actually, these were heady days for *middle-aged* Will Shakespeare: In 1604, Shakespeare was forty and had twelve years left to live.

Acutely aware of the process of aging and the inevitability of death (he called it "that dark spirit" in *Coriolanus*), Shakespeare was a theater man who had always lived life on the knife's edge of mortality with every performance. He knew that an actor's performance can do one of two things onstage: It can "kill" or it can "die." People talk about the risks inherent in other jobs—fire fighters, soldiers, Navy SEALS, childcare providers—well, with all due respect to those dedicated and tireless public servants, they've never dodged fruits and vegetables hurled by an angry audience. They've never endured the withering public put-downs of theater critics. They've never suffered the torturous shuffling and coughing of a restless and bored audience. Those of us who toil and sweat in the theater, putting ourselves in harm's way up on that stage *every single day*, recognize death as a constant companion. And Shakespeare knew it, too.

Professionally, Shakespeare was at the top of his game. In his own words "smooth success [had been strewn] before [his] feet" (from *Antony and Cleopatra*.) He had "lived to see inherited [his] very wishes" (from *Coriolanus*.) Shakespeare was "A hit, a very palpable hit!" (from *Hamlet*.) And he had become a "strumpet-mouthed coxcomb who mock'd the rudeliest dunghill with a peevish naughty buttock" (from the random order in which our magnetic Shakespeare poetry landed when it fell off the table).

He was the author (in 1604) of twenty-seven plays. He would write (or contribute to) ten more plays in his final dozen years, but only three of them (*King Lear*, *Macbeth*, and *The Tempest*) could truly be considered top-drawer. He had won awards (see sidebar on page 35).

Poems? What do you like? The man wrote two long poems, one of which ("Venus and Adonis") was more popular in his lifetime than any of the great plays we revere today. He also wrote two short poems (known in the trade as *poemlettes*[20]) and 154 sonnets that were models of concision and express thoughts of love with more depth and complexity than many of today's popular boy bands.

He also had some small fame as an actor. We've mentioned Robert Greene's dismissal of him as a mere "player"; but his name also appears on lists of actors from both 1594 and 1598; and his first biographer Nicolas Rowe wrote in 1709 that Shakespeare's "best" role was the Ghost of Hamlet's father.

Like all bald actors, Shakespeare was often relegated to playing old men, which may very well have been the thing to spur him on to write plays, so that he might create characters on the page he'd never be allowed to play on the stage.[21]

In addition to, and probably because of his artistic work, Shakespeare had risen in the ranks of management. Clearly he was held in much esteem by his "ffellowes," probably because he proved so valuable by writing plays. Theater, like television now, is a beast that must be fed; actors performed, and audiences consumed new scripts, at an alarming rate. Quality was less of an

---

[20] We think.

[21] Another compensation was that, fortunately, like all bald men, Shakespeare was swaggeringly well-endowed.

THE OLDEN GLOBE AWARDS

Movies have the Oscars®. Broadway has the Tonys®. London has the Olivier Awards (patent pending). And Elizabethan Theater had the Olden Globes®. William Shakespeare and his plays won more Olden Globes than any other Elizabethan playwright. Check out this partial list:

Best Special Effects: *The Tempest*

Best Supporting Actress: Samuel Gilburne as Juliet, *Romeo and Juliet*

Best Racist Stereotype: Shylock, *The Merchant of Venice*

Best Stage Direction: "Exit, pursued by Bear." *The Winter's Tale*

Best Product Placement: "There is a Tide in the affairs of men." *Julius Caesar*

Best Tongue-Twister: "If it were done when 'tis done, then 'twere well it were done quickly. If the assassination could trammel up the consequence, and catch, with his, success." *Macbeth*

Best Insult: "Thou whoreson obscene greasy tallow-catch!" *Henry IV, Part 1*

Best Insult (Runner-up): "Stale old mouse-eaten dry cheese." *Troilius and Cressida*

Best Pickup Line: "A good heart, Kate, is the sun and the moon; or, rather, the sun, and not the moon; for it shines bright and never changes, but keeps his course truly. If thou would have such a one, take me; and take me, take a soldier; take a soldier, take a king." *Henry V*

Most Concise Prediction of Results of Successful Pickup Line: "I'll have her, but I will not keep her long." *Richard III*

Most Unmemorable Title: *Henry VI, Part 3*

Best Scene-Stealing Role: Lucio, *Measure for Measure*

Play Most Likely to Have Audience Stand and Cheer: *Hamlet*

Play Most Likely to Put Audience to Sleep: *Henry VI, Part 1*

Role with Longest Time to Sleep Offstage in Dressing Room: Cordelia, *King Lear*

issue than quantity (hmm, also like television now, come to think of it), but not only did Shakespeare's plays prove to be some of the most popular in the repertoire, he could also churn them out quickly, writing two or three a year if modern dating is correct (and there's every reason to believe it isn't).

Clearly the Burbage brothers knew a good thing when they saw it, and we can surmise that they made Shakespeare an attractive offer. Rather than be paid for each script on a play-by-play basis, it's probable that Shakespeare was offered part ownership of the Chamberlain's Men, in exchange for which he'd continue to act and—more importantly—continue to write plays. "And they better be goddamn money spinners that'll revolutionize theater as we know it and outlive us all," growled Burbage as he gulped down his ale and groped a serving wench.[22]

The Chamberlain's Men were successful and had the problems that all successful companies have. They had to program plays that would sell tickets so they could pay their people. Then, as they continued to succeed and grow, they had to find larger quarters to accommodate the numbers of people who wanted to see them. And they had to combat government censorship and, sometimes, public opinion. It's funny to think of theater as an emerging technology but, like the Internet and television (damn that recurring analogy!), in the 1600s, theater was brand-new and people didn't know what its impact would be.

Fortunately, on her best days (which were many) Queen Elizabeth knew that theater could be a unifying agent of change and a force for good.

Not everybody felt that way, of course. The Puritans wanted to close the theaters down (and bringing down the wrath of God in the form of the plague certainly did the trick, at least for a while). When the Chamberlain's Men tried to build a new indoor theater in Blackfriars, a fashionable middle-class district on the north side of the Thames, they were met with resistance from the locals who feared that a theater in their midst would attract

---

[22] This has been a dramatic re-enactment. No actual serving wenches were groped during its writing. All wench action was monitored by the People for the Ethical Treatment of Wenches and the Wench Humane Society.

the wrong sort of person. They changed their tune when the Chamberlain's Men became the King's Men under James I. It's amazing how dropping the right name opens doors.

Meanwhile, Burbage's twenty-two-year-old lease to the Theater expired in 1598 and wasn't going to be renewed. (Sorry, we should clarify: Burbage had a lease to the *land* on which the *building* named "the Theater" sat; he didn't have a lease to all of theater. Obviously, one man can't be said to hold the lease on an entire art form.[23] Don't feel too stupid: see "Art Thou Bound for the Theater?" [page 38], Shakespeare's long-lost comedy sketch which made Elizabethan hay of this very confusion.) Fortunately, a loophole in the lease made it clear that although Burbage and his partners didn't own the land, they did in fact own the building itself and were legally allowed to do with it as they pleased. So on December 28, 1598, under cover of darkness (to avoid hired thugs preventing them physically from doing what they were allowed to do legally), the Chamberlain's Men—Shakespeare very likely among them—took the building apart board by board, loaded it onto wagons, shlepped it across the Thames, and reassembled it as a brand-new theater not far from the Rose.

They called it the Globe.

They had a thirty-one-year lease on the land, and Shakespeare had a one-tenth share in the theater, becoming one of history's first "shareholders." William Shakespeare: poetic genius, marketing genius, and financial genius.

Fig. 9. Shakespeare's Globe.

Professionally, therefore, Shakespeare was doing quite well. Personally, however, Shakespeare was torn up inside.[24] Unless he was a total jerk, he must have been a tiny bit conflicted about the family he was ignoring up in Stratford.

---

[23] Unless you're talking Zamfir, Master of the Pan Flute. That guy's got it locked up.

[24] We say this because it's a gross oversimplification, completely unsupported by any facts, and the basest sort of wild speculation. We stand by it.

The long-lost sketch

"Art Thou Bound for the Theater?"

by William Shakespeare

Friar Abbott: *Art thou bound for the Theater?*

Petruchio Costello: *Aye, verily. I'm bound for the Rose.*

Abbott: *Thou art bound for the Theater?*

Costello: *Aye, my Lord. 'Tis the Rose for which I'm bound.*

Abbott: *Good sir, I remain confused. Thou sayest thou art not bound for the Theater.*

Costello: *Sir, you remain witless and deaf. The theater is my destination. I'm bound for the Rose!*

Abbott: *But not the Theater.*

Costello: *Aye, the theater, thou addle-pated clotpoll! What strange malady possesseth thee? I'm going to the Rose Theater!*

Abbott: *Ah, I now perceive that we might have been at cross-purposes. I ask if you're going to the Theater, Burbage's specifically named playhouse.*

Costello: *(laughing) I mistook you, sir. I thought you were using the term in its generic derivation, meaning the art form, not the building therein where said art form is practiced. I thought thou maintained some foul malevolence towards the Rose.*

Abbott: *No, sir. The Rose, by any other name, would be as swell a place to see a show as any other I could devise.*

Costello: *(scratching his ass, deeply) But sir, how knew thou I wast going to a theater?*

Abbott: *I discerned that thou wast already picking out thy seat.*

It's appealing to think that perhaps Shakespeare sent money to his family. Money is, after all, one of the few things we know for a stone-cold certainty that Shakespeare coveted. Hmm...that being the case, Shakespeare probably *didn't* send money to his family in Stratford.

Maybe Shakespeare, despite his artistic and financial success, remained unfulfilled. Perhaps it wasn't theatrical greatness that motivated him, but his family's lack of social standing. Maybe the Dark Lady found a younger poet, one with more hair (and thus, tinier genitals). Whatever the reasons (and despite the evidence), scholars believe that Shakespeare moved back to Stratford, sometime around 1610. He kept his toe in the London waters—new productions here, real-estate dealings there—but he seems to have spent his last six years completely focused on fulfilling his—and by implication, his father's—lifelong dream of living and dying a country gentleman.

"Seems, Madam?" Shakespeare wrote in *Hamlet*. "Nay it is. I know not 'seems.'" Really? Is that what really happened?

If Shakespeare spent his final years at his writing table, composing elegies and writing his memoirs so that his legacy and methodology could be spelled out to an anxious and waiting world, it's clear that he also must have spent even more time at the fireplace, destroying his elegies and memoirs because no writings of any kind in the master's own hand still exist.[25]

At this point the seasoned Shakespearean biographer has no choice but to construct a likely scenario for Shakespeare's final days. Here's ours:

Shakespeare retired to Stratford under the guise of living out his life as a country gentleman. But in his true heart of hearts, Shakespeare remained what he always had been: a showman. He knew instinctively how to entertain an audience, how to divert them, frighten them, how to sustain tension, how to release it

---

[25] There is one section of the play *Sir Thomas More* written by someone scholars refer to as "Hand D," that is, the fourth distinct handwriting in the manuscript. Scholars generally agree that this is Shakespeare's handwriting. If so, it's the one remnant of his writing he neglected to destroy.

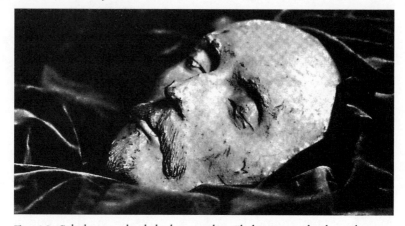

Fig. 10. Scholars are divided: this is either Shakespeare's death mask or an audience member sleeping through *Henry VI, Part 3.*

with moments of laughter, how to confound expectations, how to shock and surprise, and more important, how to keep an audience coming back for more.

So he did all that and more with his own legacy. Rather than leave around a bunch of workbooks, first drafts, unfinished projects, or any correspondence, he destroyed it all. Everything he ever wrote. Maybe he left one copy of each play to Hemminges and Condell to publish in the First Folio.

FUN FACT:
Did you know that if Shakespeare were alive today, he'd be kicking and screaming inside his coffin?

Because Shakespeare knew—like movie stars know; like reclusive authors such as J. D. Salinger know—that people can't resist mystery. Mystery adds an aura of the unknowable, a patina of the possible. Mystery creates a relationship with the reader: It's an invitation to keep searching, keep exploring, dig deeper, in the hopes that one day the answer will be revealed. If answers were easily forthcoming, people would move on and lose interest, stop searching, stop exploring. It's a good trick: Always leave your audience wanting more.

Shakespeare consciously created the mystery of his own legacy by destroying all evidence of it. That's the kind of genius he was, the kind who could see the future and his own place in it, and who could create the burning desire to know him and understand him by denying us any insight into his life. That way, our focus would remain more properly on his work, where it belongs. That's our scenario, anyway, and we're sticking to it

ESSAY QUESTION: *What are the odds? The Chamberlain's Men built the Globe Theater just down the road from today's Shakespeare's Globe Theater, which was reconstructed from meticulous archaeological research and opened in 1997. How cool is that? Give examples.*

POP QUIZ, HOTSHOT: *In his will, Shakespeare left small bequests to pay for memorial rings to which of his following "ffellowes"?*

    A. Richard Burbage
    B. John Hemminges
    C. Henry Condell
    D. All of the above

Famed Beatle drummer Ringo Starr's real name is:

    A. Richard Burbage
    B. Richard Starkey
    C. Richard III
    D. All of the above.

First Answer: B & C

Second Answer: D. No, just kidding, B.

Just the Facts, Ma'am

The facts of Shakespeare's life are very simple and are listed here. You can see that this simple, bare-bones list, all by it-self, would be one of the world's thinnest books and not very entertaining (or profitable). This explains all the pages sur-rounding this one, which have been gathered together for your reading pleasure and to justify the outrageous cover price, thank you very much.

• 26 April 1564 — Baby Shakespeare is christened. He's listed in the parish register as *Gulielmus Shakspere*. His nickname in-spires Bobby Sherman's 1970s hit, "Gulie Gulie Gulie, Do Ya Love Me?"

• Between 1564 and 1582—18 years—we got *bupkis*. The record of Shakespeare's childish actions and youthful indiscre-tions has been wiped clean. Lucky guy: if only that were true for the rest of us.

• 27 November 1582 — *Willelmum Shaxpere* marries *Annam Whateley*, according to the Episcopal register of the Worcester diocese. Willelmum (today we know he was *William*) was eigh-teen; Annam (today we know she was *Already Knocked-Up*) was twenty-six.

• The very next day, the bond is posted for the marriage of a certain *William Shagspere* to *Anne Hathwey*. Scholars assume *Wil-lelum* and *Annam* and *William* and *Anne* are the same couple. Scholars will buy anything.

• Late May 1583, only six months after the wedding, a daugh-ter is born. On 26 May, she's christened *Oops* until cooler heads prevail and change her name to *Susanna*.

• Late January 1585, the twins are born and baptized on 2 Feb-ruary. *Judith* and *Hamnet* are named after Shakespeare's good friends Judith and Hamnet Sadler. The basis of their friendship is unknown, but can you say *Elizabethan wife swapping*? Without spitting?

• Seven years go by, during which nothing about Shakespeare is known. In more than 400 years of digging, not a shred of documentary evidence about where Shakespeare was between 1585 and 1592 or what he was doing has turned up. Scholars consider this lack of evidence irrefutable proof of Shakespeare's genius.

• 1592 — Shakespeare pops back up on the grid. He's alluded to by Robert Greene in A Groats-worth of Wit (quoted earlier):

> ... there is an upstart crow, beautified with our feathers, that with his Tiger's heart wrapped in a player's hide, supposes he is as well able to bombast out a blank verse as the best of you: and being an absolute Johannes fac totum, is in his own conceit the only Shake-scene in a country.

There are four allusions (or *illusions* if you remain super dubious) to Shakespeare here: the "tiger's heart" business paraphrases a line in Henry VI, Part 3; "wrapped in a player's hide" seems to refer to an actor who's writing on the side; Johannes fac totum is Latin for Johnny know-it-all or jack-of-all-trades, which by all accounts Shakespeare was; and of course the punny reference to William's last name: Shakes-scene.

• Interestingly, Henry Chettle, the editor of Groats-worth, later prints a retraction in which he apologizes and tries to clarify that he was referring to somebody else, not Shakespeare.[26]

• 18 April 1593 — "Venus and Adonis" is registered with the Stationers Company (sort of like an Elizabethan copyright office, except that it gave all rights to the printer/publisher instead of the author) by Richard Field, a man from Stratford who might have been a friend of Shakespeare. The name "William Shakespeare" appears, not on the title page, but at the end of the dedication to the Earl of Southampton. As far as we know, this is the first appearance of the name "William Shakespeare" anywhere in print. But again, as we've said, we're idiots.

• 1594 — Another poem, "The Rape of Lucrece," is published.

---

[26] Bert Fields, in *Players: The Mysterious Identity of William Shakespeare*, makes quite a meal of this whole Groats-worth business, alleging (among other things) that Chettle might have written Groats-worth himself; that the whole paragraph might refer to the famous actor Edward Alleyn; and that somebody very highly placed in society or the government must have put pressure on Chettle to apologize (which would imply that "Shakespeare" was somebody with friends in high places, like the Earl of Oxford or somebody). Jesus, some people just won't let things go.

Clearly Shakespeare is in a poem- and sonnet-writing frenzy, so scholars conclude he had to have been getting some hot-and-heavy romantic action. (Or not. Seriously, what makes people write poems? What's the point?)

• Also in 1594 — Shakespeare is listed for the first time as an actor with the Lord Chamberlain's Company. Although there's no evidence of this, as an actor he would also have been highly skilled at waiting tables.

• 1596 — Big year for Bill:

    † A man sues Shakespeare and several others, craving "sureties of the peace" against him; meaning this man would prefer that Shakespeare and his buddies not beat the crap out of him. Apparently Shakespeare, along with his many other achievements, also invented the modern-day hooligan.

    † Shakespeare's name appears in the tax records of St. Helen's Parish, Bishopsgate, London.

    † Shakespeare applies for and is granted a coat of arms, the ultimate Elizabethan status symbol (sort of like an iPod, but, if you can believe it, even cooler). Both Shakespeare and his father (who applied for it first and was denied) are now granted the right to append the title "Gentleman" after their names. Shakespeare is apparently thinking of that "upstart crow" crack when he chooses the family motto *Non sans droit*, which is French for "Nonsense duck."[27]

    † Shakespeare's son Hamnet dies. Scholars believe this event inspired Shakespeare to write his great tragedy *Hamlet*. Unfortunately, around the same time, Shakespeare also wrote two zippy comedies, *Much Ado About Nothing* and *Merry Wives of Windsor*, so it's just possible that scholars (if you haven't figured it out by now) don't know what the hell they're talking about.

---

[27] Others translate this as "Not without right." We report, you decide.

• 1597 — Shakespeare buys New Place, formerly owned by the Lord Mayor of London and the second-largest house in Stratford. It costs "a bundle," which in today's money would be "a buttload."

• 1598 — Shakespeare's name is mentioned twice: as being interested in the purchase of some land; and as one of the chief holders of grain in the Stratford area—this during a time of great shortage. Poetic genius? Absolutely. Philanthropist and humanitarian? Not so much.

• Also in 1598, Shakespeare is listed as an actor in Ben Jonson's *Every Man in His Humor*. Interestingly (and this is absolutely true) in the sequel *Every Man Out of His Humor*, Ben Jonson seems to refer to Shakespeare's fabulous new coat of arms by having a pompous character refer to his own new personal motto "Not without mustard." Did Shakespeare find this funny? Good question. Do you?

• 1599 — Shakespeare is made one-tenth owner of the Globe Theater. The Burbage brothers split half, while Shakespeare and four other players (John Hemminges, Augustine Phillips, Thomas Pope, and Will Kemp) split the other half. The third half is given to fellow player Henry Condell, who's too stupid to realize there's no such thing as a third half and kicks himself till the end of his days.

• 1601 — John Shakespeare dies. Shakespeare writes *All's Well That Ends Well*. Coincidence? You decide.

• March 13, 1602 — Shakespeare is mentioned in a bawdy diary entry by a law student who writes of Richard Burbage, by then so famous an actor, that when a female admirer arranged a rendezvous with him, she told him to announce himself as Richard III (his most famous role) and she would let him in. "Shakespeare, overhearing their conclusion," (according to this diary entry) beat Burbage to the lady's chambers and was "at his game" before Burbage arrived. When Burbage announced that "Richard III" was there, Shakespeare called from inside, "William the Conqueror comes before Richard the Third," proving that sometimes the pen and the sword can be mighty *at exactly the same time.*

• 1602 — Shakespeare pays £320 (almost a quarter of a million dollars in today's money—seriously) for some farmland in Straford. Where'd that money come from? How much money did Shakespeare actually make from all his writings? How much money did Shakespeare make from his various real-estate holdings? How much money did Shakespeare make for fronting for the Earl of Rutland?[28] These are all good questions.

• 1603 — King James accedes to the throne and becomes the new patron of Shakespeare's acting company, which now becomes known as the King's Men. (The actors had to have been disappointed, as the king's second choice, the James Gang, was infinitely cooler.)

• 1604 — Shakespeare and eight other players receive an allotment of red cloth to make ceremonial robes for King James's coronation. There's enough left over for some bitchin' curtains.

• 1604 — Shakespeare sues a neighbor for thirty-five pounds and ten pence; in 1608 he sues another man for six pounds. (The pound Sterling was—and still is—the English monetary unit: Shakespeare was looking for money here, not quantities of flesh.)

• 1605 — Shakespeare buys the right to collect tithes on the produce of his fellow Stratfordians; in other words, the right to profit from other people's labor. This sounds incredibly archaic and medieval, but think of it this way: It's like when Michael Jackson bought the rights to, and started collecting royalties from, all of the Beatles' old songs. The irony is that Shakespeare was ultimately forced to sell his tithing rights, also like Michael Jackson, in order to pay off his enormous legal debts.[29]

• 1608 — Shakespeare becomes one-sixth owner of the theater at Blackfriars, the indoor winter venue for the King's Men. This time, Henry Condell is let in on the deal. His descendants rejoice.

• 1612 — Shakespeare gives a deposition in a London trial. The great playwright's kind of showing himself to be a litigious

---

[28] The Earl of Rutland will be discussed in Part Five. Go there now, if you're impatient. We'll wait.

[29] The eerie Michael Jackson/William Shakespeare parallels continue: Shakespeare's working title for *The Tempest* was *Thriller*.

courthouse groupie in his later years, isn't he? Especially for a guy who once wrote "First thing we do, let's kill all the lawyers." Same old story, man: Success changes you.

• 1613 — Shakespeare buys and mortgages the gatehouse of the Blackfriars theater. Did he live there? Nobody knows, but most scholars think he was living in Stratford at this time. Was it for the rental income? Possibly. More probable is that it was an in-town trysting place for Shakespeare, since Shakespeare—genius though he undoubtedly was—had yet to invent the automobile and its roomy backseat.

• 1613 — Speaking of the Earl of Rutland, Shakespeare is paid forty-four shillings by the sixth earl, Roger Manners's son Francis, to help create an "impresa," a painted shield that was displayed at tournaments and fancy events. Richard Burbage was paid, too, "for paynting and making it," so Shakespeare probably just wrote the text. We're guessing that because he was paid in gold, the Earl of Rutland came off looking like quite the fellow.

• Also in 1613, the Globe Theater in London burns down. A cannon going off in the first scene of Shakespeare's final play, *Henry VIII*, probably started the fire, making Shakespeare the first playwright in the history of theater to literally bring down the house.[30]

• 1616 — William Shakespeare writes the most confusing document that still exists with his name attached: his will. In it, he's described as "William Shackspere of Stratford-upon-Avon in the county of Warwick gentleman." Clearly, this "gentleman" business is more important to him than this "posthumous-world-renown-as-a-playwright-slash-poetic-genius" business, seeing as how his will mentions absolutely nothing at all connected to the world of letters: no books, no old manuscripts, no unfinished works, no nothing. Which is fine; maybe he didn't think much of it, maybe his papers weren't all that important to him, maybe he had no idea he was going to have such a fabulously famous afterlife so he just included all his books and papers under the phrases "all my remaining property," or "all the rest of my goodes and

---

[30] Sorry. That joke was mandated by guild rules.

chattels" (which he left to his daughter Susanna and her husband). That makes sense, but clearly he thought more of being a "gentleman" than he did about being a "husband." Shakespeare not only lived in London writing sonnets, writing and acting in plays, and wooing Dark Ladies for most of his marriage, but also left his wife one thing and one thing only when he died: their "second best bed." What a guy.

- 1616 — William Shakespeare dies.
- 1623 — The First Folio is published.[31]
- 1623 to the Present — William Shakespeare lives happily ever after.

---

[31] The what? What's a "First Folio"? Relax, we'll get to it.

THE PLAYS OF
WILLIAM SHAKESPEARE

"The play's the thing."
Hamlet, Act II, Scene 2

 ll right, we've covered Shakespeare's life, but there's a reason Shakespeare never wrote, "The *playwright's* the thing."

That's because the *plays* are the things: huge, overlong, with stolen, convoluted plotlines, but also filled with some of the greatest poetry and most unforgettable characters ever to step out onto a stage.

The first published collection of Shakespeare's plays is called the First Folio of 1623. It was assembled by Shakespeare's friends and theatrical colleagues John Hemminges and Henry Condell as a loving tribute to their late friend (whose death was making him even later) and as a way to make a quick farthing.[32] The First Folio contains thirty-six of Shakespeare's

Fig. 11. Genius at work. Shakespeare absentmindedly scribbling on his thigh.

---

[32] Shakespeare left money in his will to Hemminges and Condell to purchase some commemorative rings. Maybe this was his thanks to them. Maybe Shakespeare suggested the Complete Works volume to them before he died. Maybe we have no idea and we're just guessing.

SIZE MATTERS!

As with so many things, in the case of the First Folio and Quartos, it's the size that's important. Okay, take an ordinary piece of paper. Now fold it in half. That's the way they folded the sheets of paper in the First Folio. Now take that same sheet of folded paper and fold it one more time. That's the way they folded the paper in the Quartos—into *quarters*, get it? Got it? Good.

plays, but doesn't include *Pericles*, *Two Noble Kinsmen*, or *Cardenio*.[33]

Eighteen of Shakespeare's plays had been published individually before the First Folio in what were called Quarto editions. Some of these were authorized, but a handful of them weren't and may have been partly cobbled together using a combination of actual script pages and actors' memories.

Since the First Folio, the canon has been traditionally organized into Comedies, Histories, and Tragedies.[34] This is simple and elegant, but an absolute pain in the *tuchis* if you're looking up one of the plays and have forgotten that King Lear is not a real English king, whether Macbeth is historical or tragic (the guy's historical; the play's tragic), whether *Taming of the Shrew* is funny or tragic (depends on your feelings for Kate), or are completely confused by *Comedy of Errors* because the title tells you it's supposed to be funny but you've read it or seen it and know that it's not.

We're going to list the plays several different ways: first by their First Folio designation, then according to their more recent categorization, then in the approximate chronological order in

---

[33] Interestingly, it also doesn't contain *Death of a Salesman*.

[34] Why Shakespeare's thirty-nine plays have been traditionally referred to as "the Canon" is a mystery. Evidence suggests it derives from Shakespeare's frequent pickup line, "Hey babe, wanna see my canon?"

which they were written, then finally in alphabetical order, which is by far the easiest way to look them up, and why nobody else lists them this way remains a mystery. It's just part of our commitment to making this the easiest reference book for the serious and dedicated Shakespearean scholar who really isn't all that bright.

The Plays as Listed in the First Folio

They appear under the heading "A Catalogve of the feuerall Comedies, Hiftories, and Tragedies contained in this volume."[35] Note that not all of Shakespeare's thirty-nine plays appear in the First Folio.

The Comedies

The Tempest
The Two Gentlemen of Verona
The Merry Wives of Windsor
Measure for Measure
The Comedy of Errors
Much Ado About Nothing
Love's Labour's Lost
A Midsummer Night's Dream
The Merchant of Venice
As You Like It
The Taming of the Shrew
All's Well That Ends Well
Twelfth Night, or What You Will

The Tragedies

The Tragedy of Coriolanus
Titus Andronicus
Romeo and Juliet
Timon of Athens
The Life and Death
   of Julius Caesar
The Tragedy of Macbeth
The Tragedy of Hamlet

King Lear
Othello, the Moor of Venice
Antony and Cleopatra
Cymbeline, King of Britain

The Histories

The Life and Death of King John
The Life and Death of Richard
   the Second
The First Part of King Henry
   the Fourth
The Second Part of Henry
   the Fourth
The Life of King Henry the Fifth
The First Part of Henry the Sixth
The Second Part of Henry
   the Sixth
The Third Part of Henry the Sixth
The Life and Death of Richard
   the Third
The Life of King Henry the Eighth

---

[35] Hmmm, this Elizabethan typo theory is looking more convincing all the time.

THE HISTORIES

There is general agreement that Shakespeare wrote ten plays that are classified as Histories. They deal with the history of England and are based on fact, but Shakespeare took many liberties in order to make the plays more dramatic. In some cases this worked. In others, such as the plays *King John* and *Henry VIII*, he managed to eliminate most of the really juicy historical fact and ended up with some pretty crappy plays.

You see, in Shakespeare's day, theater was allowed at the king or queen's pleasure. The monarch could say "yea" or "nay" to pretty much anything. So it behooved Shakespeare to smooch a little royal behind and write plays that showed the royal ancestors in a very good light. By all accounts, Shakespeare was an expert kisser in this regard. Though virtually all his playwrighting contemporaries served time in jail for displeasing the authorities, Shakespeare himself was never sent to the slammer. That was the good news. The bad news is that in order to keep the monarch happy, Shakespeare trod lightly in places where there was potentially great dramatic material. Like, for instance, the six wives of Elizabeth I's father, Henry VIII. Showing the messy divorces and deaths of Henry's wives might have sold a lot of tickets, but at what cost? Undoubtedly, Shakespeare had no desire to end up in the Tower of London as the girlfriend of a Beefeater.

So here's the deal: In cases where the queen's ancestors were good guys, Shakespeare could dramatize that and write wonderful plays, like *Henry V*. In cases where the historical king was an enemy of the queen's ancestors, Shakespeare could write them as villains, and these, too, could be wonderful, like *Richard III*.

Where Shakespeare ran into dramatic difficulty was when he had to depict bad kings in a good light to keep on the current regime's good side. This is how you end up with a play as uncharacteristically bad as *Henry VIII*.[36]

A couple of other points about the Histories: In the late 1990s, several major Shakespeare publishers added *Edward III* to their lists of Shakespeare's Histories. The authorship of this play has been in dispute for hundreds of years. It did not appear in the First Folio or in *Palladis Tamia* by Francis Meres, published in 1598, which listed Shakespeare's early works. Computer analysis, however, indicates that it's likely Shakespeare wrote one scene in the play.[37] Nonetheless, we're not going to include *Edward III* as one of Shakespeare's Histories. Why not? He wrote *one scene!* (Maybe.) So it doesn't count! And this book's getting too long as it is.

We should also point out that several of Shakespeare's Tragedies are based just as much on real historic figures as his Histories. Macbeth was a real person, as was Julius Caesar, as were Antony and Cleopatra, as was King Lear, as was Cymbeline. Now hang on, this gets confusing. The reason the plays based on these

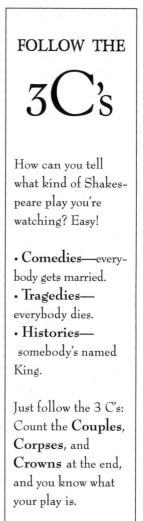

FOLLOW THE

3C's

How can you tell what kind of Shakespeare play you're watching? Easy!

- **Comedies**—everybody gets married.
- **Tragedies**—everybody dies.
- **Histories**—somebody's named King.

Just follow the 3 C's: Count the **Couples**, **Corpses**, and **Crowns** at the end, and you know what your play is.

---

[36] In Shakespeare's defense, some scholars argue that *Henry VIII* was actually written by somebody else and that Shakespeare only contributed a handful of scenes. Listen, if you're going to have a play listed in your Folio, you can't then say, "Hey, I never saw that play before!" If you can't take the critical heat, stay out of the playwright's kitchen.

[37] This raises the question, "How reliable are computers?" Co-author Austin Tichenor signed up for a computer dating service and was matched with a series of real losers. Co-author Reed Martin once had his handwriting analyzed by a computer at a county fair that said he would end up cynical and bitter. Maybe these are bad examples.

historic figures are labeled Tragedies rather than Histories is simply that Shakespeare took such great liberties with the facts in order to dramatize their stories that the plays aren't historically accurate. No, wait. The History plays are just as historically inaccurate as the Tragedies, so that's not the reason. The reason that some plays based on historical figures are listed as Tragedies and others as Histories is that in the Tragedies these real figures die at the end and in the Histories they don't. No, wait. The title characters die at the end in lots of Shakespeare's histories—*Richard II*, *King John*, *Henry IV, Part 2*, and *Richard III*.

So we guess the reason these plays are listed as Tragedies is . . . oh, who are we kidding? There is no reason. It's just random, okay? Like the universe itself. Get over it. Quit trying to analyze everything to death. Some of the Tragedies are just as historic (which is to say hardly historically accurate at all) as the History plays. So there. We said it. Let's move on.

The sources for most of Shakespeare's Histories (and several of his Tragedies, but please, can we not go there again?) are Raphael Holinshed's *The Chronicles of England, Scotland and Ireland* (1586-87), and Edward Hall's *The Union of the Two Noble and Illustre Families of Lancaster and York* (1548).

If you're in a really, really big hurry, here's a very short plot synopsis of all the History plays. They're all pretty much the same. Here it is:

An English king (usually named Henry, sometimes Richard, and once John) is fighting the French. At the same time, someone at home is trying to take over the throne of England from the reigning king.

That's it. Any questions? No? Good.

ESSAY QUESTION: *You are a seventeenth-century playwright and would like to live to a ripe old age. Would you write history plays that show the current monarch in a positive or negative light? Why?*

THE COMEDIES

Let's get something straight. Shakespeare wrote nineteen Comedies. Not thirteen Comedies, plus six Romances. Not ten Comedies, plus six Romances, plus three Problem Plays. It's nineteen Comedies. Nineteen. Count 'em.

How do we know this? Because in the First Folio, Shakespeare's buddies, Hemminges and Condell, didn't have any plays listed as either Romances or Problem plays. And the First Folio is always right.[38]

Wussy Shakespeare apologists came up with terms like "Romance" and "Problem Play" to try to excuse the fact that some of Shakespeare's comedies aren't funny. And some are sad.

And some deal with very serious issues. And, yes, some are just plain bad. But such is the nature of comedy: Some of it is sad, like certain films of Charlie Chaplin and Buster Keaton. Some great comedy deals with serious issues, like *One Flew Over the Cuckoo's Nest* and *Dr. Strangelove*. And, yes, some comedy *is* just bad, like the work of Carrot Top or Shakespeare's *All's Well That Ends Well*. (Wow. Those are two things we never expected to see in the same sentence.)

Now that we've established the number of Shakespearean Comedies, let's distinguish them from the Histories and Tragedies. In a word, Comedies end on a *hopeful* note, as opposed to the Tragedies, in which the title character always ends up dead. And the Histories, which are based on real historic figures (as are some of the Tragedies, but please, please someone make us *stop!*).

And another thing: As well as being hopeful, Shakespeare's Comedies usually feature at least one character who is a crossdresser. Remember, Shakespeare was English, and nothing is funnier to an Englishman than a guy in drag. (No, we don't understand it either.)

---

[38] Except, of course, when it's wrong. The First Folio doesn't even list *Pericles, Cardenio, or Two Noble Kinsmen,* which are now accepted as proud members of the Shakespearean canon.

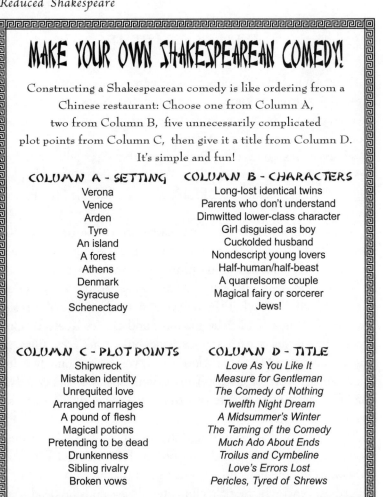

MAKE YOUR OWN SHAKESPEAREAN COMEDY!

Constructing a Shakespearean comedy is like ordering from a
Chinese restaurant: Choose one from Column A,
two from Column B, five unnecessarily complicated
plot points from Column C, then give it a title from Column D.
It's simple and fun!

COLUMN A - SETTING

Verona
Venice
Arden
Tyre
An island
A forest
Athens
Denmark
Syracuse
Schenectady

COLUMN B - CHARACTERS

Long-lost identical twins
Parents who don't understand
Dimwitted lower-class character
Girl disguised as boy
Cuckolded husband
Nondescript young lovers
Half-human/half-beast
A quarrelsome couple
Magical fairy or sorcerer
Jews!

COLUMN C - PLOT POINTS

Shipwreck
Mistaken identity
Unrequited love
Arranged marriages
A pound of flesh
Magical potions
Pretending to be dead
Drunkenness
Sibling rivalry
Broken vows

COLUMN D - TITLE

Love As You Like It
Measure for Gentleman
The Comedy of Nothing
Twelfth Night Dream
A Midsummer's Winter
The Taming of the Comedy
Much Ado About Ends
Troilus and Cymbeline
Love's Errors Lost
Pericles, Tyred of Shrews

Oh, yeah. And a shipwreck. Lots of shipwrecks in Shakespeare's
Comedies. What could be funnier than tragedy at sea? Can you
imagine what fun Shakespeare would have had with *Titanic*?

Identical twins who get mistaken for each another are big. As
are forests and young lovers. And parents that just don't understand. And a wedding.

We're not saying that Shakespeare's comedies are formulaic . . .
no, wait a minute, that's exactly what we're saying. And we've
got no problem with that because it works. The art of most of

the great comedians was formulaic. Remember that movie where Charlie Chaplin played a tramp? Or the time that Jack Benny was stingy and played the violin? How about that episode of *Gilligan's Island* where the castaways were trying to get home? Or the episode of *Seinfeld* that wasn't really about anything at all? Or that Marx Brothers' movie where Harpo is silent and plays the harp, while Chico does a bad Italian accent and plays the piano, and where Groucho goes around insulting everybody? That's right. They were like that in pretty much every movie or episode in which you saw them. And you loved them for it.

THE TRAGEDIES

Most of Shakespeare's greatest plays were Tragedies. They are the stories of great men whose downfall is caused by a character flaw. Macbeth's flaw is that he is overly ambitious and easily influenced. Hamlet's flaw is that he is indecisive. Titus Andronicus's flaw is that he is the title character of a really terrible play.

Most of Shakespeare's Tragedies are loosely based on real historic figures. This is completely different from Shakespeare's Histories, which are loosely based on real historic figures. (Don't get us started.) There were real people named Julius Caesar, Antony and Cleopatra, King Cymbeline, King Lear, Macbeth, Titus Andronicus, and Coriolanus. There was even a prince of Denmark named Amleth. Really.

Not to give too much away, but in Shakespeare's tragedies you know going in that the title character is going to die by the end of Act V. In some cases, as in *Timon of Athens*, you find yourself hoping that he'll die in Act II so the play will end and you can go home. But in most cases, knowing the ending does not diminish the experience. It's like the movie *Titanic*. You knew from the title that the ship was going down, but you still enjoyed watching Leonardo DiCaprio freeze to death.

Whereas the Comedies deal with resolving conflict and celebrating the continuity of life, the Tragedies deal with the inflexibility of society and the inevitability of fate.

The Plays by Category
(According to more recent scholarship)

Note that *Cymbeline, King of Britain* has been redesignated as a Romance;[39] that some of Shakespeare's lesser-known works like *Pericles, Troilus and Cressida*, and his various poems have been added; and that despite its wacky anti-Semitic, Jew-baiting antics, *The Merchant of Venice* is still inexplicably listed as a Comedy.

The Comedies
Two Gentlemen of Verona
The Taming of the Shrew
The Comedy of Errors
Love's Labour's Lost
A Midsummer Night's Dream
The Merchant of Venice
The Merry Wives of Windsor
Much Ado About Nothing
As You Like It
Twelfth Night
Troilus and Cressida
All's Well That Ends Well
Measure for Measure

The Histories
King John
Richard II
Henry IV, Part 1
Henry IV, Part 2
Henry V
Henry VI, Part 1
Henry VI, Part 2
Henry VI, Part 3
Richard III
Henry VIII

The Tragedies
Titus Andronicus
Romeo and Juliet
Julius Caesar
Hamlet
Othello

Timon of Athens
King Lear
Macbeth
Antony and Cleopatra
Coriolanus

The Mysteries
The Hound of The Baskervilles
The Maltese Falcon
What Women Want
Who Wrote Shakespeare

The Poems
The Sonnets
A Lover's Complaint
Venus and Adonis
The Rape of Lucrece
The Phoenix and the Turtle
Other Poems Too Shortz, Insignificant,
   or Undiscovered to Mention

The Romances
Pericles
Cymbeline
The Winter's Tale
The Tempest
Cardenio
Two Noble Kinsmen

The Flintstones
Fred
Wilma
Pebbles

---

[39] Despite our adamant insistence there was no such category about five pages back.

The Plays Chronologically

Note that this is the approximate order in which the plays were written (according to the best scholarship available), *not* the order in which the plays take place. (Compiling that list would take scholars geekier than we are.) Note that *Henry VI, Part 1* was written after parts 2 and 3, as a kind of prequel. Note also the distinct lack of jokes, for which we apologize.

Two Gentlemen of Verona	1590	Julius Caesar	1599
The Taming of the Shrew	1590-1	As You Like It	1600
Henry VI, Part 2	1591	Hamlet	1600-1
Henry VI, Part 3	1591	Twelfth Night	1601
Titus Andronicus	1592	Troilus and Cressida	1602
Henry VI, Part 1	1592	All's Well That Ends Well	1603
The Comedy of Errors	1592	Measure for Measure	1604
Richard III	1592	Othello	1604
Love's Labour's Lost	1593	Timon of Athens	1605
Romeo and Juliet	1594-5	King Lear	1605-6
A Midsummer Night's Dream	1595	Macbeth	1606
Richard II	1595	Antony and Cleopatra	1607
The Merchant of Venice	1596	Pericles	1607
King John	1596	Coriolanus	1608
Henry IV, Part 1	1597	Cymbeline	1609
Henry IV, Part 2	1597-8	The Winter's Tale	1610-1
The Merry Wives of Windsor	1597-8	The Tempest	1611
Much Ado About Nothing	1598	Cardenio	1612-3
Henry V	1599	Henry VIII	1613
		Two Noble Kinsmen	1613-4

Fig. 12. Six men and a dog, searching for the source of Shakespeare's genius.

The Plays Alphabetically

The following pages provide synopses, settings, and sources for each play, as well as the important facts each person should really know if they want to think of themselves as well read and semi-intelligent. They could also help you win bar bets, so pay attention.

All's Well That Ends Well

Antony and Cleopatra

As You Like It

Cardenio

Comedy of Errors, The

Coriolanus

Cymbeline

Hamlet

Henry IV, Part 1

Henry IV, Part 2

Henry V

Henry VI, Part 1

Henry VI, Part 2

Henry VI, Part 3

Henry VIII

Julius Caesar

King John

King Lear

Love's Labour's Lost

Macbeth

Measure for Measure

Merchant of Venice, The

Merry Wives of Windsor, The

Midsummer Night's Dream, A

Much Ado About Nothing

Othello

Pericles

Richard II

Richard III

Romeo and Juliet

Taming of the Shrew, The

Tempest, The

Timon of Athens

Titus Andronicus

Troilus and Cressida

Twelfth Night

Two Gentlemen of Verona

Two Noble Kinsmen

Winter's Tale, The

ALL'S WELL THAT ENDS WELL (1602) *Comedy/Problem Play*

Setting: Roussillon (wherever that is)

Source: *The Decameron* by Giovanni Boccaccio.

Best Known For: Being of dubious merit and its use of the "bed-trick," in which a woman tricks a man into becoming her husband.

Major Characters:

Helen—In love with Bertram

Bertram—The Count of Roussillon (wherever that is . . . okay, it's in France), not in love with Helena

Plot: Helena is in love with Bertram, who is not in love with her. The good news is that she saves the life of the king of France and he tells her that she can choose anyone she wants to marry. She picks Bertram. He thinks he's above her but has to agree to the marriage. Helena returns to Roussillon (it's in France—everyone knows that!), thinking that Bertram will be along shortly, but he takes off for Tuscany, where he falls for Diana. But with the help of Diana, Helena entraps Bertram. Just before Bertram and Diana go to bed together, Helena and Diana switch places in the dark. Helena gets pregnant by Bertram, and they all live happily ever after.

One-Sentence Plot Encapsulation: All is not well that ends well, and this play doesn't.

Moral: Do it with the lights on.

Famous Quote: You'd think there would be one other than the title, but there isn't.

Best Feature: Helena tricking Bertram into getting her pregnant. It's like an Elizabethan episode of *Jerry Springer.*

Worst Feature: This is considered one of Shakespeare's "problem plays." The main "problem" is that it's a comedy that isn't particularly funny.

Rating (on a scale of one to five "Bards"):

Interesting Fact: Some critics believe that *All's Well That Ends Well* is a reworked version of a play called *Love's Labour's Won*, one of Shakespeare's "lost plays." Not all scholars agree: In fact, our favorite Shakespearean expert, Dr. Peter Holland, remains Scooby-Dubious.

> **ESSAY QUESTION:** *Have you ever had sexual relations with a partner who thought that you were somebody else? Explain.*

ANTONY AND CLEOPATRA (1607) *Tragedy*

Setting: Ancient Egypt

Source: Plutarch's *The Lives of Noble Greeks and Romans.*

Best Known For: Cleopatra killing herself with the bite of an asp.

Major Characters:

Antony—One of the three rulers of Rome.

Cleopatra—Queen of Egypt.

Plot: Antony goes to Egypt to question Cleopatra about recent events. He falls madly in love with her and starts to ignore matters of state. This leads to trouble back in Rome, so Antony returns there. In an attempt to patch up political problems, he marries Caesar's sister. Cleopatra learns about the marriage and is furious. She swears to win Antony back. Meanwhile, relations between Caesar and Antony worsen and they go to war. Antony has returned to Egypt to be with Cleopatra, and she insists on commanding the Egyptian fleet in the upcoming battle with Caesar. But when the time comes, she flees and all her boats follow her home. Needless to say, Antony is furious and threatens to kill Cleopatra. To protect herself, Cleopatra sends word to Antony that she is dead. In sadness, Antony stabs himself, but before he dies he gets word that Cleopatra is not really dead. He is carried to her side where he dies in her arms. Cleopatra then holds a poisonous snake to her breast that bites and kills her.

One-Sentence Plot Encapsulation: Love bites.

Moral: Never get involved in Middle Eastern affairs.

Famous Quotes:

"My salad days, when I was green in judgment." Act I, Scene 5

"I have immortal longings in me." Act V, Scene 2

Best Feature: This play is full of wonderful poetry.

Worst Feature: The play is all over the place—very hard to follow.

Rating:

Interesting Facts: *Antony and Cleopatra* has more scenes than any other Shakespearean play. There are two different TV film versions, each boasting supporting performances by actors from *The Fresh Prince of Bel-Air.* Strange, but true. Who knew?

> **ESSAY QUESTION:** *Do you prefer Shakespeare's Comedies or Tragedies? Which do you think are funnier?*

As You Like It (1600) *Comedy*

Setting: The forest of Arden, England

Source: *Rosalynde* by Thomas Lodge.

Best Known For: The "All the world's a stage" speech in Act II, which describes the "seven ages of man."

Major Characters:

Oliver and Orlando—Brothers

Rosalind—Daughter of Duke Senior

Celia—Daughter of Duke Frederick

Duke Senior—Former ruler whose throne was usurped.

Duke Frederick—Duke Senior's evil brother who did the usurping.

Plot: Duke Frederick has usurped the throne from his brother, Duke Senior, who now lives in the Forest of Arden. Meanwhile, Oliver tries to get his brother's—Orlando's—neck broken in a wrestling match, but Orlando wins the match instead and along the way catches the eye of Rosalind. The evil Duke banishes Rosalind, and her good friend Celia joins her in the forest of Arden, where Rosalind dresses up like a boy to hide her identity (and Celia, in an even bolder disguise, dresses up as a slightly different girl). Orlando also leaves for the forest so that Oliver won't have another opportunity to try to kill him. Once there, he hangs love poems to Rosalind on the trees, where she finds them and learns that Orlando loves her. Still dressed as a boy, she tells Orlando that she will cure him of this love by "pretending" to be Rosalind and rejecting him. Meanwhile, Oliver has followed Orlando to the forest. Orlando saves him from being killed by a lion, and they reconcile. Rosalind reveals herself to Orlando. They plan to be married, as do Celia and Oliver. Finally, evil Duke Frederick decides to go live in a monastery and gives the throne back to his brother.

One-Sentence Plot Encapsulation: *Desperate Houswives* set in the forest of Arden.

Moral: You can always get your guy by pretending to be a boy. Huh?

Famous Quotes:

"*Neither rhyme nor reason*" Act III, Scene 2

"*For ever and a day*" Act IV, Scene 1

"*All the world's a stage,*

And all the men and women merely players.

They have their exits and their entrances;

And one man in his time plays many parts…" Act II, Scene 7

Best Feature: One of Shakespeare's best comedies

Worst Feature: At this point in his career, Shakespeare had been using the "girls dressing up like boys" gimmick for over a decade.

Rating: 💀 💀 💀 💀

Interesting Fact: Shakespeare grew up near the real Forest of Arden in Warwickshire, England. It was named after his ancestors on his mother's side.

ESSAY QUESTION: *In this comedy, Oliver asks a wrestler to break his brother's neck. Explain why this is funny.*

CARDENIO (1612–3) *Comedy/Romance*

Source: Miguel de Cervantes's *Don Quixote*.

Best Known For: Being a "lost" Shakespeare play. No definitive text exists.

Major Characters (probably):

Govianus—King, all around good guy

The Lady—His love

The Tyrant—Bad guy

Plot: Well, the play is lost so . . . something along the lines of the Tyrant trying to take over the throne and steal the girl. Eventually, he fails at both.

One-Sentence Plot Encapsulation: Good triumphs over evil, but the fair lady dies in the process.

Moral: Back up your hard disk.

Famous Quote: Um, no

Best Feature: The mystery surrounding the play's existence.

Worst Feature: Apparently there is no character named Cardenio in the play. Really.

Rating: Zero Bards

Interesting Fact: Shakespeare is supposed to have collaborated with John Fletcher on this play. The British Museum owns what may be a prompt book for *Cardenio* used by Shakespeare's company.

> **ESSAY QUESTION:** *Do you think Shakespeare tried the excuse, "The dog ate* Cardenio"?

THE COMEDY OF ERRORS (1592) *Comedy*

Setting: Ephesus

Source: The Roman Comedies *Menaechmi* and *Amphitruo* by Plautus.

Best Known For: Two pairs of identical twins who get mistaken for each other.

Major Characters:

Antipholus of Syracuse and Antipholus of Ephesus—Identical twins.

Dromio of Syracuse and Dromio of Ephesus—Their servants, the other identical twins

Egeon—Father of the two Antipholuses

Plot: The twins have been separated as children. Fast-forward thirty-three years later. Antipholus of Syracuse decides to search for his long-lost brother. They both end up in the same town, where both sets of twins get mistaken for the other. Comic hijinks ensue.

One-Sentence Plot Encapsulation: Twins is funny.

Moral: Adoption is a choice, too.

Famous Quote: None.

Best Feature: This play can actually be pretty funny—there are lots of opportunities for slapstick comedy. (Of course, *Macbeth* can be pretty funny if you put lots of slapstick in it. On its own? Not so much.)

Worst Feature: Productions in which the twins look nothing alike.

Rating: 💀 💀 💀

Interesting Fact: Minneapolis and St. Paul, Minnesota, are known as the Twin Cities.

> **ESSAY QUESTION:** *Jose Canseco actually has an identical twin brother, Ozzie, who also allegedly used steroids, but only played briefly in the major leagues. What does this tell us about the actual benefits of steroid use for baseball players?*

CORIOLANUS (1608) *Tragedy*

Setting: Rome 491–487 BC

Source: Plutarch's *The Life of Caius Martius Coriolanus*.

Major Characters:

Coriolanus

Plot: Coriolanus is a great warrior but also aloof. He has no sympathy for the lower classes. Lots of fighting, then he gets killed.

One-Sentence Plot Encapsulation: Coriolanus dies.

Moral: People skills matter.

Famous Quote: None.

Best Feature: Nobody performs it much.

Worst Feature: You name it.

Rating: 💀

Interesting Fact: None.

CYMBELINE (1609) Comedy/Romance

Setting: Ancient Britain

Source: *Cymbeline* seems to be one of the few Shakespearean plays where he didn't steal the basic plot from someone else. Apparently, he thought this one up himself. We should be grateful he didn't do it more often.

Best Known For: Not being very well known.

Major Characters:

Cymbeline—King of Britain

Imogen—His daughter

Queen—An evil queen

Posthumus—Becomes Imogen's husband

Cloten—Cymbeline's step-son, a bad guy

Iachimo—Another bad guy

Plot: King Cymbeline wants his daughter, Imogen, to marry his stepson, Cloten, but she marries Posthumus instead, so Cymbeline banishes Posthumus. Posthumus goes to Rome, where Iachimo bets him that he can seduce Imogen. Iachimo doesn't succeed in seducing her, so he sneaks into her bedroom when she is asleep and takes notes about her body, which he then relays to Posthumus, who is convinced of Imogen's betrayal. Posthumus orders his servant to kill Imogen. This is called hiring a hit man. The servant can't bring himself to kill our heroine, so he takes her to Milford Haven and disguises her as a . . .wait for it . . . a man! Cloten has followed Imogen to Milford Haven and then gets his head cut off. The evil queen sends her servant to give medicine, which she thinks is poison, to either Imogen or Posthumus. She isn't too particular. If either one dies, her son — Cloten — will be in line for the throne. Except that he's dead. And she doesn't know that yet. But now Imogen sees Cloten's headless body and thinks it's Posthumus's body because Cloten was wearing Posthumus's clothes to fool Imogen. It works.

Now the evil queen gets really sick, and on her deathbed confesses all her evil deeds. Then there's some silly stuff about a war between Britain and Rome. But it all works out. Posthumus and Imogen get back together, and they all live happily ever after. Did you follow any of that?

One-Sentence Plot Encapsulation: The play is really about Imogen, not Cymbeline.

Moral: Don't marry an evil queen. Don't bet someone that they can't seduce your wife. Don't let someone cut off your head. All good advice.

Famous Quotes:

"The game is up" Act III, Scene 3

"I have not slept one wink" Act III, Scene 4

Best Feature: With a wicked queen giving the beautiful girl a potion that makes it look like she's dead, if Shakespeare had just added seven dwarves, this would have been a Disney classic.

Worst Feature: No dwarves.

Rating: 🎭🎭

Interesting Fact: The word *Cymbeline* sort of rhymes with *gabardine*.

ESSAY QUESTION: *Why would anyone put on this play? Seriously.*

HAMLET *(1600) Tragedy*

Setting: Denmark

Source: German play *Hystorie of Hamblet*, Francois de Belleforest's *Histoires Tragiques*, and an earlier play from the 1500s (probably by Thomas Kyd) titled *Hamlet*, which scholars call Ur-*Hamlet*. Please don't ask why. You don't want to know.

Best Known For: Hamlet holding a skull and asking, "To be, or not to be."

Major Characters:

Hamlet—Prince of Denmark

The Ghost of Hamlet's Father

Gertrude—Hamlet's mother

Claudius—King of Denmark

Plot: Hamlet's father, the King of Denmark, has recently died. Hamlet's mother, Gertrude, quickly marries her dead husband's brother, Claudius. Hamlet's dead father appears as a ghost, tells Hamlet that he has been murdered by Claudius, and asks Hamlet to avenge his death. Hamlet spends the rest of the play trying to decide whether or not to kill Claudius.

One-Sentence Plot Encapsulation: Hamlet avenges his father, and it only takes four hours.

Moral: He who hesitates is lost. Fish or cut bait. Poop or get off the pot.

Famous Quotes: Almost too many to name:

"To be, or not to be: that is the question . . ." Act III, Scene 1

"To thine own self be true." Act I, Scene 3

"Brevity is the soul of wit." Act II, Scene 2

"Alas, poor Yorick! I knew him, Horatio." Act V, Scene 1

"Neither a borrower nor a lender be." Act I, Scene 3

"Something is rotten in the state of Denmark." Act I, Scene 4

"The rest is silence." Act V, Scene 2

TO BE OR NOT TO BE IN SHAKESPEARE'S PLAYS

To Be	Not to Be
Julius Caesar	Orange Julius
Hermia	Hernia
Richard II	Little Richard
Timon of Athens	Timon of Fresno
Henry IV, Parts 1 & 2	George Bush, Parts 1 and 2
Macbeth	Mac the Knife
Mistress Quickly	Sir Premature
Joan of Arc	Joan Van Ark
Caliban	Taliban
Gonerill	Chlymidia
Speed	Heroin
Touchstone	Warner Bros.
Don John	Don Johnson
Fabian	Frankie Avalon
Cassius	Muhammad Ali
Brutus	Popeye
Rosencrantz and Guildenstern	Rhoda Morgenstern
Mark Antony	Jennifer Lopez
Cassio	Sony
Portia	Porsche

Best Feature: In all likelihood, this is the greatest play ever written.

Worst Feature: Other than that, it's terrible

Rating: 💀 💀 💀 💀 💀

Interesting Fact: Shakespeare's son, Hamnet, died in his youth shortly before Shakespeare wrote this play.

> **ESSAY QUESTION:** *Are people from Denmark Dutch or Danish? Can you ever keep that straight? How?*

HENRY IV, PART 1 (1597) *History*

Setting: England, circa 1400

Source: Holinshed's *Chronicles*.

Best Known For: Being one of Shakespeare's best History plays.

Major Characters:

King Henry IV—Killed Richard II and is feeling guilty

Prince Hal, his son—First shown sowing his wild oats, he later becomes Henry V

Hotspur (real name: Henry Percy)—Brave and a real hothead.

Sir John Falstaff—Prince Hal's best friend; a fat, old, alcoholic knight

Plot: Prince Hal, heir to the throne, spends his days drinking and whoring with his friend Sir John Falstaff, to the dismay of his father, King Henry IV. The Percy family is mad at King Henry IV, so they put together a rebel force to overthrow him. Prince Hal, who up until this point is known for his waywardness, suddenly grows up. He goes to battle, saves his father's life, and defeats Hotspur.

One-Sentence Plot Encapsulation: Same as in *The Lion King*: princes have to grow up.

Moral: Same as in *The Lion King*: Hakuna matata.

Famous Quotes:

"The better part of valour is discretion." Act V, Scene 4

"It's the circle of life." Act I

Best Feature: Sir John Falstaff, probably Shakespeare's greatest comic creation (next to Pumbaa from *The Lion King*).

Worst Feature: Confusing title. The play is really about Prince Hal, not his father, Henry IV.

Rating: 💀 💀 💀 💀 💀

Interesting Fact: More has been written about the character Falstaff than any other Shakespearean character except Hamlet.

> **ESSAY QUESTION:** *As a young man, Prince Hal shirks responsibility and drinks too much, while his father runs a powerful nation. Hal grows up, cleans up his act, and ends up ruling the country himself. Can you draw any parallels between Prince Hal, King Henry, and a recent American presidential dynasty? Why not? What's wrong with you?*

HENRY IV, PART 2 (1597–8) History

Setting: England, early 1400s

Source: Holinshed's *Chronicles.*

Major Characters:

King Henry IV—England's monarch

Prince Hal, later King Henry V

Sir John Falstaff—Prince Hal's best friend and worst influence.

Plot: King Henry IV's army defeats the rebels. Shortly thereafter, the king dies. Prince Hal becomes the new king. Falstaff seeks favors from his old pal who is now ruler of England, but the new king turns him away.

One-Sentence Plot Encapsulation: Prince Hal's movin' on up.

Moral: Don't forget the little people who got you where you are.

Famous Quote:

"Uneasy lies the head that wears a crown." Act III, Scene 1.

Best Feature: More of Falstaff.

Worst Feature: It's a sequel. Draw your own conclusions.

Rating: 💀 💀

Interesting fact: Reno, Nevada, is farther west than San Diego, California. (Oh. You wanted an interesting fact about *Henry IV, Part 2*? Hey, who doesn't?)

ESSAY QUESTION: *Does the sequel* Henry IV, Part 2 *have more in common with* Godfather II *or* Rocky II? *Why?*

HENRY V *(1599) History*
 Setting: England, early 1400s
 Source: Holinshed's *Chronicles.*
 Best Known For: Stirring British patriotism in times of war.
 Major Characters:
 King Henry V—Formerly Prince Hal
 The Archbishop of Canterbury—Leader of the Church of England
 The Dauphin—Heir to the French throne
 Katherine—Daughter of the King of France
 Plot: The Archbishop of Canterbury convinces Henry V to lay claim to France. The Dauphin then insults Henry V by sending him some tennis balls. (Really. If you'd read the play or seen the movie, you'd know this.) Henry V decides to invade France although he is outmanned five to one. He gives a rousing speech to his army, the English win the battle of Agincourt, Henry V marries Princess Katherine of France, and the two historic enemies are united in peace.
 One-Sentence Plot Encapsulation: A king's gotta do what a king's gotta do.
 Moral: England good. France bad.
 Famous Quotes:
 "Once more unto the breach, dear friends . . . " Act III, Scene 1
 "We few, we happy few, we band of brothers . . . " Act IV, Scene 3
 Best Feature: This is the dirtiest of all the history plays. It's got lots of bawdy innuendo and wordplay.
 Worst Feature: King Henry V's pageboy haircut.
 Rating: 💀 💀 💀 💀
 Interesting Fact: *Henry V* is the only one of Shakespeare's history plays in which nobody is trying to oust the king of England. (They are, however, trying to overthrow France.)

ESSAY QUESTION: *Of Shakespeare's ten history plays, seven have a King Henry in the title. Could this possibly be more confusing? How?*

HENRY VI, PART 1 *(1592) History*

   Setting: England, beginning in 1422
   Source: Holinshed's *Chronicles.*
   Best Known For: Not being very good.
   Major Characters:
   King Henry VI
   Charles, the French Dauphin—Heir to the French throne.
   Henry Beauford—Bishop of Winchester, generally bad guy.
   Joan of Arc—Sainted French heroine or schizophrenic troublemaker, depending on who you ask.
   Duke of Gloucester—Protector of England and the king.
   Plot: As the play begins, the great King Henry V has just died. Henry VI is too young to become king. The English and the French are fighting, blah, blah, blah. Some English nobles are mad at the king and decide to help the French. Henry is torn between marrying for duty or love. He marries for love. To be continued . . .
   One-Sentence Plot Encapsulation: Henry V—both the play and the king—is a tough act to follow.
   Moral: Not even a genius can hit it out of the park every time.
   Famous Quote: Are you kidding? There are none.
   Best Feature: When the play drags, as it does frequently, you can imagine an actual dolphin playing the role of the French dauphin.
   Worst Feature: Two sequels. It's as if someone felt the need to make *Ishtar II* and *Ishtar III*.
   Rating: 💀
   Interesting Fact: It's thought that Shakespeare collaborated with Thomas Nashe in writing *Henry IV, Part 1*. It was apparently their only collaboration, thank goodness.

ESSAY QUESTION: *Why can't the English and the French just get along?*

HENRY VI, PART 2 *(1591)History*
  Setting: England, 1400s
  Source: Holinshed's *Chronicles.*
  Best Known For: Being no better than *Henry VI, Part 1.*
  Major Characters:
  King Henry VI
  Duke of Gloucester—The king's uncle.
  Queen Margaret—The king's wife.
  Plot: The Yorks are leading a rebellion against King Henry. By the end of the play, nothing is resolved but the Yorks have a slight advantage. To be continued . . .
  One-Sentence Plot Encapsulation: Like a cricket match and Celine Dion's love, these plays will go on.
  Moral: Too much of a good thing is dangerous. Too much of a *bad* thing is twelve hours out of your life you'll never get back.
  Famous Quote:
  "First thing we do, let's kill all the lawyers." Act IV, Scene 2
  Best Feature: One good quote (see above).
  Worst Feature: The rest of the play.
  Rating: 🖤
  Interesting Fact: Shakespeare wrote *Henry VI, Parts 2* and *3* before he wrote *Part 1*

ESSAY QUESTION: *George Lucas's* Star Wars *prequels were clearly inspired by* Henry VI, Part 1 *because they're of such similar quality. Discuss.*

HENRY VI, PART 3 *(1591) History*
  Setting: England, mid 1400s
  Source: Holinshed's *Chronicles* and Hall's *Union.*
  Best Known For: Being no better than the first two parts of the *Henry VI* trilogy.

Major Characters: The usual suspects; see *Henry VI, Parts 1* and *2*.

Plot: The House of York finally wins the day. Henry VI is stabbed to death.

One-Sentence Plot Encapsulation: The play so nice, he wrote it thrice!

Moral: It's important to know when to stop.

Famous Quote:
"The smallest worm will turn, being trodden on." Act II, Scene 2.

Best Feature: This play marks the end of the seemingly endless *Henry VI* trilogy.

Worst Feature: Masochists are disappointed that it's finally over.

Rating: 💀

Interesting Fact: Some critics believe this play is deeply flawed and that it demonstrates that Shakespeare was growing weary of the subject matter. These critics are correct.

ESSAY QUESTION: *Do you personally know anyone named King Henry? What's she like?*

HENRY VIII (1613) *History*

Setting: England, 1520–33

Source: Holinshed's *Chronicles*.

Best Known For: Strangely, this play is not well known for anything despite being about one of England's most famous kings.

Major Characters:

King Henry VIII—King of England

Cardinal Wolsey—His chief advisor

Queen Katharine—Wife of Henry VIII

Anne Bullen[40]—Lady-in-waiting to Queen Katharine, who later becomes queen herself.

---

[40] Yes, this is the wife better known nowadays as Anne Boleyn. Shakespeare spelled it the way he pronounced it.

Plot: Henry has been married to Katharine for twenty years, but does not have a male heir. At a party, he is smitten with Anne Bullen and asks the Pope for an annulment of his marriage, ostensibly because Queen Katharine is the widow of his brother. The Pope refuses to annul the marriage, and Cardinal Wolsey is wrapped up in the whole mess. Henry VIII divorces Katharine and marries Anne Bullen. Wolsey dies. Queen Katharine dies. Queen Anne Bullen has a daughter by Henry VIII, whom they name Elizabeth. She will grow up to be Queen Elizabeth I.

One-Sentence Plot Encapsulation: Henry wants a son and will stop at nothing to get one.

Moral: Divorce is a pain in the neck.

Famous Quote: "I'm her eighth old man called Henry / Henry the eighth I am." (Herman's Hermits)

Best Feature: It's rarely performed today.

Worst Feature: It's occasionally performed today.

Rating: 💀

Interesting Fact: Shakespeare was able to take one of the most interesting figures in English history and write an extremely uninteresting play about him. This can be attributed to the fact that either Shakespeare didn't write the entire play himself (he collaborated with John Fletcher), or more likely to the fact that Henry VIII's grandson, James I, was Shakespeare's patron, so the Bard felt compelled to portray the title character in something of a good light.

> **ESSAY QUESTION:** *The Globe Theater burned to the ground on June 29, 1613. Henry VIII was performed in the theater that day. Legend has it that the theater's thatched roof was set ablaze by cannons fired during the performance. What does this teach us about arms control?*

JULIUS CAESAR (1599) *Tragedy*

Setting: Ancient Rome

Source of the Play: Plutarch's *Lives*.

Source of Fiber: A diet rich in fruits and vegetables.

Best Known For: The "Friends, Romans, countrymen" speech delivered by Mark Antony.

Major Characters:

Julius Caesar—Roman ruler and military hero

Brutus—A man of integrity

Cassius—Plotter against Caesar

Mark Antony—Caesar's friend

Plot: Cassius is jealous of Julius Caesar and plots his overthrow. He gets others, including Brutus, to join him by convincing them that Caesar's growing power is a threat to democracy. The conspirators murder Caesar in the Senate. Mark Antony vows revenge on the murderers. Brutus and Cassius flee Rome and put together an army, but they constantly bicker. In Philippi, which is in Greece, the forces of Brutus and Cassius meet to fight the army of Mark Antony. Cassius accidentally kills himself. Later, Brutus kills himself.

One-Sentence Plot Encapsulation: When in Rome, watch your back.

The Moral: Beware the Ides of March.

Famous Quotes:

"Et tu, Brute?" (Which translates as "Et tu, Brutus?") Act III, Scene 1

"The fault, dear Brutus, is not in the stars / But in ourselves." (which translates as "We screwed up.") Act I, Scene 2

"Friends, Romans, countrymen, lend me your ears." (which translates as, "Yo, listen up!") Act III, Scene 2

Best Feature: Togas.

Worst Feature: Shakespeare named two characters after Jennifer Lopez's lovers: Marc Antony and the third spear carrier from the left known as Caius ben Affleckus.

Rating: 💀 💀 💀 💀

Interesting Fact: In today's world it would be unthinkable to overthrow the leader of a country in order to promote democracy.

ESSAY QUESTION: *Don't you wish more current politicians would murder each other and commit suicide? Which ones? Be specific.*

KING JOHN (1594) *History*

Setting: England 1199–1216

Source: Holinshed's *Chronicles*. Also, an earlier anonymous play from 1591: *The Troublesome Reign of John, King of England*.

Best Known For: Shakespeare omitting from the play what is today considered by far the most significant part of King John's reign: The fact that he signed the Magna Carta, the precursor to the U.S. Declaration of Independence and to the U.S. Constitution. King John was also the villainous *Prince* John from the story of Robin Hood (King Richard was off fighting the Crusades). Unfortunately, that's not in this play, either, because anything would have helped.

Major Characters:

King John—King of England (succeeded his brother, Richard the Lionheart)

Arthur—The king's nephew

Philip "the Bastard" Faulconbridge (what a great name!)

Plot: King John has a weak claim to the throne. King John's nephew, Prince Arthur, believes he is the rightful king. The French back Prince Arthur's claim and try to start an English rebellion. King John invades France, with Philip the Bastard in command. They fight to a draw. The Pope orders the French to break the peace and then excommunicates King John. The English beat the French and capture Prince Arthur. King John orders Arthur's eyes to be burned out, but his captor can't bring himself to do it. Arthur tries to escape by leaping from the prison walls but falls to his death. The English and French fight again to a draw. King John is poisoned.

One-Sentence Plot Encapsulation: Give 'em an inch and they'll take a mile.

Moral: When writing a play about somebody, don't leave out the most interesting things they did.

Famous Quote: "I didn't say we were better than Jesus. I said we were more popular." (King) John Lennon

Best Feature: None.

Worst Feature: Everything. This play is terrible.

Rating: 🎭

Interesting Fact: Strangely, in 1899, *King John* became the first Shakespearean play ever made into a movie. Fortunately, nobody has ever had the urge to do it again.

FUN FACT: *King John* and *Richard II* are Shakespeare's only plays that are entirely in iambic pentameter. They contain no prose.

ESSAY QUESTION: *Do you know anyone who has actually seen the play* King John? *Why?*

KING LEAR (1605–6) *Tragedy*

Setting: Ancient Britain

Source: Holinshed's *Chronicles*.

Best Known For: Along with *Hamlet*, being Shakespeare's best work. It questions the difference between sanity and insanity, between order and chaos.

Major Characters:

King Lear—The elderly king of Britain

Regan, Cordelia, and Goneril—His three daughters

Plot: King Lear is old and wants to evenly distribute his lands among his three daughters. He asks which of his three daughters love him the most. Regan and Goneril proclaim deep love for him. Cordelia won't play this game. Lear gets mad and banishes Cordelia, while dividing his land equally between the other two daughters. But Regan and Goneril betray their father, and he goes mad. He sees Cordelia hanged and then dies himself.

One-Sentence Plot Encapsulation: Lear tries to control his daughters and ends up losing them all.

Moral: It's hell getting old.

Famous Quote:
"Blow winds, and crack your cheeks! Rage! Blow!" Act III, Scene 2

Best Feature: A major character named after a venereal disease.

Worst Feature: Watching very old actors play King Lear and wondering if they're really going to drop dead.

Rating: 💀💀💀💀💀

Interesting Fact: Shakespeare intentionally set *King Lear* in pre-Christian Britain so that the tragic ending of the play could not be explained away as the will of a loving Christian God. But really, the whole story is pretty tragic no matter who they were praying to.

FUN FACT: Productions of *Lear* were prohibited in England from 1788–1820 because the king at the time, George III, was (like Lear) just a little bit bonkers.

ESSAY QUESTION: *How far along are you in your estate planning? Do you have a will or trust?*

LOVE'S LABOUR'S LOST *(1594) Comedy*

Setting: Navarre, a kingdom between France and Spain
Source: Original.
Best Known For: Being obscure and not very funny.
Major Characters:
Ferdinand—King of Navarre
Berowne, Longaville, and Dumaine—Three Navarrean lords
Princess of France—The Princess of France
Rosaline, Maria, and Katherine—Three French ladies
Don Adriano de Armado—A fantastical Spaniard
Costard—The king of Navarre's fool

Plot: King Ferdinand and his three lords swear off women in order to focus on learning. Then the Princess of France and her three ladies arrive and all bets are off. The men disguise themselves as Russians to try and woo the ladies. (Don't ask, we don't understand it, either). Oh, yeah, and love letters are delivered to the wrong parties. Comic hijinks ensue. In a hilarious ending, the Princess of France learns that her father has died and she must return to France. She tells King Ferdinand that if he will do a year of penance in a hermitage, she'll marry him.

One-Sentence Plot Encapsulation: Are women necessary?

Moral: Don't go see this play.

Famous Quote: Mmm. Nope.

Best Feature: The comic relief provided by the characters Don Adriano de Armado and Costard.

Worst Feature: It's got lots of Elizabethan references and puns that make the play dated and hard to understand.

Rating: 🎭 🎭

Interesting fact: Of all of Shakespeare's plays, *Love's Labour's Lost* has the greatest percentage of rhyming couplets—62 percent of the text.

ESSAY QUESTION: *Co-author Reed Martin played Constable Dull in a college production of this play. Was this typecasting?*

MACBETH *(1606) Tragedy*

Setting: Scotland

Source: Holinshed's *Chronicles.*

Best Known For: Its supernatural creepiness.

Major Characters:

Macbeth—A general in the king of Scotland's army

Lady Macbeth—His wife

Three Witches

King Duncan of Scotland

Macduff—A Scottish nobleman

Plot: Macbeth, encouraged by three witches and his power-hungry wife, wants to be king of Scotland. He kills King Duncan and becomes king himself. Lady Macbeth goes mad and dies. Macbeth is then killed by Macduff.

One-Sentence Plot Encapsulation: Lady Macbeth encourages her husband to be more aggressive in pursuing career options.

Moral: What goes around comes around.

Famous Quotes:

"Out, damn'd spot!" Act V, Scene 1

"Double, double, toil and trouble;

Fire burn, and cauldron bubble" Act IV, Scene 1

"Life's but a walking shadow; a poor player,

That struts and frets his hour upon the stage,

And then is heard no more: it is a tale

Told by an idiot, full of sound and fury,

Signifying nothing." Act V, Scene 5

Best Feature: Witches.

Worst Feature: Theater people believe *Macbeth* to be cursed and will only refer to it as "the Scottish play." Most people think this is nonsense, but the evidence is overwhelming. Consider that in every single production mounted in the four hundred years since it was written, something inconvenient has occurred during rehearsals or performances. This never happens in productions of other plays. And here's the clincher: Every single actor from the original production in 1606 is now dead!

Rating:

WHAT TO DO IF YOU ACCIDENTALLY SAY "**MACBETH**" IN A THEATER

1. Step quickly outside the stage door, turn around three times, say "Thrice around the circle bound, Evil sink into the ground," and spit over your left shoulder.

2. Find a gun and blow your brains out. Anything's better than enduring the hysterical shrieks of a bunch of drama geeks.[41]

---

[41] Obviously, you should *not* blow your brains out with a gun, no matter how much those silly theater ninnies may make you want to. No, it's far better to scratch your eyes out with your own hands.

Interesting Fact: *Macbeth* is Shakespeare's shortest tragedy.

ESSAY QUESTION: *Superstitions are silly. Macbeth. There, I said it. I'll say it again: Macbeth. See? Nothing happ–. . . aak! Help, help! AAHH!*

MEASURE FOR MEASURE (1604) *Comedy/Problem Play*
Setting: Vienna
Source: *Hecatommithi* by Cinthio.
Best Known For: The hilarious scene in which Claudio begs his sister to sleep with Angelo so that Angelo won't kill him.
Major Characters:
Isabella—Virtuous sister of Claudio
Vincentio—Duke of Vienna
Claudio—Isabella's brother
Lord Angelo—The Duke's deputy
Plot: It's all very simple. The duke decides to take a sabbatical from ruling and appoints Angelo to be in charge in his absence. The duke asks him to more strongly enforce morality laws. But the duke hangs around town disguised as a monk to see how everything goes. Angelo arrests Claudio and sentences him to death for impregnating his fiancée. Isabella pleads with Angelo to spare her brother's life. Angelo says that if Isabella will sleep with him, he will pardon Claudio. She refuses and tells her brother what happened. He tries to convince her to sleep with Angelo to save his own life. The duke overhears this conversation and hatches a scheme to resolve everything. He tells Isabella to accept Angelo's proposal, but then switches places with Angelo's former fiancée just before the moment of truth. The scheme works, except that Angelo decides to kill Claudio anyway. The duke finds out about this and orders that a truly guilty man be executed instead of Claudio. Isabella thinks Claudio is dead and seeks redress from the duke. The duke reveals that he was the "monk" and Angelo begs for mercy. Everyone finds out that Claudio is still alive, and the duke tells Angelo to marry his former fiancée. He also tells Claudio to marry his now pregnant fiancée, while the duke himself plans

to marry Isabella. Did we say simple? We meant simply confusing.

One-Sentence Plot Encapsulation: Dukes suck.

Moral: Don't get someone else to do your dirty work.

Famous Quote:

"What's mine is yours and what is yours is mine." Act V, Scene 1

Best Feature: Lots of sex.

Worst Feature: It's another one of those not-very-funny comedies.

Rating: 💀💀💀

Interesting Fact: This story is based on a real incident that happened in Italy in 1547.

> **ESSAY QUESTION:** *Have you ever been to Italy? Did anything like this happen to you while you were there?*

THE MERCHANT OF VENICE (1596) *Comedy*

Setting: Oh, let's say Venice.

Source: Unknown.

Best Known For: Being politically incorrect in its depiction of the Jewish moneylender, Shylock. And there's the requisite cross-dressing.

Major Characters:

Antonio—The titular merchant of Venice

Bassanio—Antonio's pal and Portia's suitor

Shylock—A Jewish moneylender

Portia—A wealthy heiress

Plot: Antonio borrows money from Shylock to pay for Bassanio's trip to woo Portia. Antonio agrees that he will forfeit a pound of flesh as the penalty if he does not pay back the loan in time. Bassanio is allowed to marry Portia because he correctly chooses which of three caskets contains her picture. (Don't ask.) Antonio's ships don't get back to Venice in time, so he can't pay back Shylock on schedule. Antonio's friends offer to pay back the loan, but Shylock insists on collecting the pound of flesh—as anyone would. Now, Bassanio gets back and offers to pay Shylock three times what he's owed, but Shylock still wants his pound of flesh. Portia pretends to be a lawyer and argues Antonio's case in court. She tells Shylock that he can take the pound of flesh, but that the agreement did not mention blood. Suddenly, Shylock decides that taking the money isn't such a bad idea. As a penalty for conspiring to kill Antonio, Portia orders Shylock to split his wealth between the duke and Antonio. And he must convert to Christianity. And they all live happily ever after.

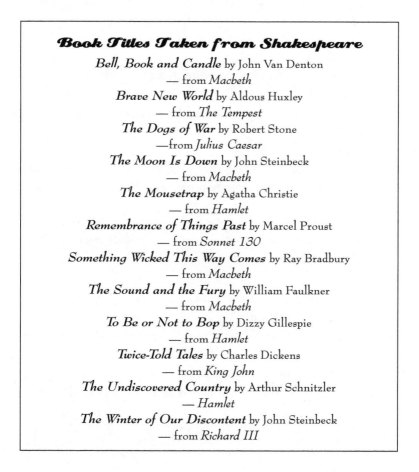

Book Titles Taken from Shakespeare

Bell, Book and Candle by John Van Denton
— from *Macbeth*

Brave New World by Aldous Huxley
— from *The Tempest*

The Dogs of War by Robert Stone
—from *Julius Caesar*

The Moon Is Down by John Steinbeck
— from *Macbeth*

The Mousetrap by Agatha Christie
— from *Hamlet*

Remembrance of Things Past by Marcel Proust
— from *Sonnet 130*

Something Wicked This Way Comes by Ray Bradbury
— from *Macbeth*

The Sound and the Fury by William Faulkner
— from *Macbeth*

To Be or Not to Bop by Dizzy Gillespie
— from *Hamlet*

Twice-Told Tales by Charles Dickens
— from *King John*

The Undiscovered Country by Arthur Schnitzler
— *Hamlet*

The Winter of Our Discontent by John Steinbeck
— from *Richard III*

One-(Long)-Sentence Plot Encapsulation: This is Shakespeare's hugely controversial play in which a Jew won't let his daughter marry a gentile (all of whom are depicted as jerks, anyway) and is just one more example of Shakespeare's liberal, secular-humanist, anti-Christian agenda.

Moral: Always read your loan papers before you sign them.

Famous Quotes:

"All that glisters is not gold." Act II, Scene 6. (No, that's not a typo. Shakespeare wrote "glisters" even though we now usually quote it as "glistens.")

"I am a Jew. Hath not a Jew eyes? Hath not a Jew hands, organs, dimensions, senses, affections, passions?" Act III, Scene 1.

"The quality of mercy is not strain'd,

It droppeth as the gentle rain from heaven

Upon the place beneath. It is twice blest:

It blesseth him that gives and him that takes." Act IV, Scene 1

Best Feature: Shylock's "Hath not a Jew eyes" speech.

Worst Feature: Anti-Semitism. Oh, yeah, that's right. It's not really there.

Rating: 🎭🎭🎭🎭.

Interesting Fact: Unlike today, in the sixteenth century, anti-Semitism was common throughout the world.

ESSAY QUESTION: *Interestingly, this play is classified as a comedy although it isn't funny. Discuss the parallels between* The Merchant of Venice *and the work of Carrot Top.*[42]

THE MERRY WIVES OF WINDSOR *(1597–8) Comedy*

Setting: We're thinking Windsor.

Source: The *Henry IV* plays and *Il Pecorone* by Ser Giovanni Fiorentino.

Best Known For: Revisiting the tremendously popular character of Sir John Falstaff, who we first met in *Henry IV, Part 1*.

---

[42] This is a truly Shakespearean joke: In four hundred years scholars will be wondering, "Who the hell was Carrot Top?" (Note to Ed.: This is our second derogatory Carrot Top reference. How many are we allowed?)

As many as you want. – Ed.

Major Characters:

Falstaff—A fat, drunken knight and scoundrel

Mistress Ford and Mistress Page—Pals

Plot: Falstaff is running out of money, so he decides to seduce both Mistress Page and Mistress Ford so he can have access to their husbands' wealth. The two ladies quickly figure out what he is up to and decide to have some fun with him. Hilarity ensues. Eventually, the ladies decide they've had enough fun, reveal the truth, and Falstaff is forgiven.

One-Sentence Plot Encapsulation: Prequel to *Dirty Rotten Scoundrels*.

Moral: Don't mess with the ladies.

Famous Quote: "This is the short and long of it." Act II, Scene 2.

Best Feature: More of Falstaff, a truly great comic character.

Worst Feature: It's a sequel, but not a bad one as sequels go. Actually, you could say that's it's more of a spin-off than a sequel. Think of *Henry IV, Part 1* as *Cheers*, and *Merry Wives of Windsor* as *Fraser*. They liked Fraser so much on *Cheers* that they gave him his own show. Shakespeare did the same with Falstaff.

Rating: 💀💀💀

Interesting Fact: It's said that Elizabeth I enjoyed the character of Falstaff so much in *Henry IV, Part 1* that she asked Shakespeare to write another play about him. (This could well be more of an interesting *story* than an actual fact. It's an idea that wasn't even recorded until more than a century after the play was written.)

> **ESSAY QUESTION:** *In this play, the husbands find out that Falstaff was trying to seduce their wives and take their money, but they forgive him in the end. If this play were an episode of* COPS, *how would it end?*

Shakespearean Quotes

Which three quotes are not from Shakespeare?

1. "We are such stuff as dreams are made on."
2. "If you prick us, do we not bleed?
   If you tickle us, do we not laugh?
   If you poison us, do we not die?"
3. "Beware the Ides of March."
4. "If the glove don't fit, you must acquit."
5. "Romeo, Romeo! Wherefore art thou, Romeo?"
6. "To be, or not to be. That is the question."
7. "A horse! A horse! My kingdom for a horse!"
8. "Blow wind and crack your cheeks!"
9. "Who let the dogs out?"
10. "Neither a borrower, nor a lender be."
11. "All that glisters is not gold."
12. "All the world's a stage and all the men
    and women merely players."
13. "If music be the food of love, play on."
14. "The Giants win the pennant! The Giants win
    the pennant!"
15. "What's in a name? That which we call a rose
    by any other name would smell as sweet."

Quotes #4, #9, and #14 are not from Shakespeare. They were obviously written by Christopher Marlowe.

A MIDSUMMER NIGHT'S DREAM (1595) Comedy

Setting: Greece

Source: None; it's one of the few completely original plays that Shakespeare wrote.

Best Known For: Being one of Shakespeare's best. It is lyrical, funny, and magical.

Major Characters:

Helena, Hermia, Demetrius, and Lysander—Young lovers

Oberon and Titania—The bickering Fairy King and Queen

Puck—Mischievous fairy

Bottom—A weaver who, along with his friends, the Rude Mechanicals, mounts a play for a royal wedding

Plot: Oberon and Titania are bickering. To distract Titania, Oberon gives Puck a magic potion to put on Titania's eyes that will make her fall in love with the first thing she sees. But the young lovers are in the forest, and Puck accidentally puts the potion in Lysander's eyes. This makes the lovers get all confused about who loves who (as you do when you're young.) The Rude Mechanicals are also in the forest rehearsing their play. Just for laughs, Puck changes Bottom's head into an ass's head. Titania has had the love potion put on her eyes, and she now awakens. The first thing she sees is Bottom, and she falls in love with him. Semibestial hijinks ensue. Oberon charms Demetrius so that he'll love Helena. Puck cures Lysander so that he'll love Hermia again. Oberon takes away the effect of the potion from Titania so that she no longer loves Bottom. Puck gets Bottom's head back to normal. The Rude Mechanicals put on their play at the royal wedding. And they all live happily ever after.

One-Sentence Plot Encapsulation: Shakespeare wrote it himself: "The course of true love never did run smooth." Act I, Scene 1.

Moral: Everybody likes a nice ass.

Famous Quote: "Lord, what fools these mortals be!" Act III, Scene 2

Best Feature: The play within the play performed by the Rude Mechanicals is usually the best part of the show.

Worst Feature: The two pairs of young lovers are not distinctively drawn. It's often hard to tell them apart.

Rating: 💀 💀 💀 💀 💀

Interesting Fact: Shakespeare never again depicted humans sleeping with animals. Somebody probably got to him.

ESSAY QUESTION: *Have you ever written a play that came to be considered one of the most significant dramas of all time? Then what right do you have to criticize Shakespeare?*

MUCH ADO ABOUT NOTHING (1598) Comedy

Setting: Italy

Source: *Novelle del Bandello* by Lucca and *Orlando Furioso* by Ludovico Ariosto.

Best Known For: The reluctant lovers, Beatrice and Benedick.

Major Characters:

Benedick—In love with Beatrice but won't admit it.

Beatrice—In love with Benedick but won't admit it.

Don John—A bastard in both senses of the word

Claudio—Gentleman in love with Hero

Hero—Cousin of Beatrice, in love with Claudio

Plot: Beatrice and Benedick are mad about each other but can't admit it, so they spar verbally. The other characters trick these two into believing that the other has declared a deep love for them. Meanwhile, Claudio and Hero are in love, but Don John and his friends conspire to break them up by convincing Claudio that Hero has been unfaithful. The plot works. At the altar, Claudio refuses to marry Hero, and she faints. Claudio thinks she's died. But the truth comes out, Don John and his accomplices are arrested, and the two happy couples get married.

One-Sentence Plot Encapsulation: People in love act like idiots.

Moral: Don't believe everything you hear.

Famous Quote: "As merry as the day is long." Act II, Scene 1

Best Feature: The hilarious fights between Beatrice and Benedick.

Worst Feature: Unfortunately, the main part of the play involves the Claudio plot, not Beatrice and Benedick.

Rating: 💀 💀 💀 💀.

Interesting Fact: Kenneth Branagh directed and starred in a film version of *Much Ado* while he was married to Oscar winner Emma Thompson. He left her for Helena Bonham Carter, who played Ophelia in Mel Gibson's film version of *Hamlet*.

ESSAY QUESTION: *Although they constantly bicker and spar, critics still consider Beatrice and Benedick one of the most mature and fully developed couples that Shakespeare created. Discuss.*

OTHELLO (1604) Tragedy

Setting: Venice

Source: Richard Knolles's *History of the Turks* (1603), and the narrative fiction of Giraldi Cinthio.

Best Known For: Being the only Shakespearean play that has a black character in the title role.

Major Characters:

Othello—A Moor and a Venetian military leader

Desdemona—Othello's wife

Iago—Othello's ensign, the bad guy

Plot: Iago is angry that Othello has bypassed him for a promotion, and also jealous of Othello's love for Desdemona. He convinces Othello that Desdemona has been unfaithful, which is untrue. Othello smothers Desdemona to death. When he discovers that Desdemona was innocent, Othello kills himself.

One-Sentence Plot Encapsulation: Othello forgoes marital counseling and takes matters into his own hands.

Moral: Take a deep breath and count to ten before killing your wife in a fit of jealous rage.

Famous Quotes: "O, beware my lord, of jealousy!
It is the green eyed monster which doth mock
The meat it feeds on." Act III, Scene 3

"She doth make the beast with two backs." Act I, Scene 1

WORDS & PHRASES

The *Oxford English Dictionary* cites Shakespeare as the earliest example of almost three thousand words in the English language. Which four words listed below are not Shakespearean?

accused

amazement

antioxidant

assassination

champion

circumstantial

compromise

critic

deafening

ebonics

frugal

generous

hint

laughable

majestic

mimic

negotiate

obscene

rant

Slurpee

torture

undress

worthless

wazzup

zany

Oh, come on! You weren't even trying! Sigh...
antioxidant, ebonics, Slurpee, and wazzup. There. Happy now?

Best Feature: Along with Richard III, Iago is perhaps Shakespeare's greatest villain.

Worst Feature: Caucasian actors attempting to play Othello.

Rating: 🗡️ 🗡️ 🗡️ 🗡️.

Interesting Fact: At the time Othello was written, Queen Elizabeth was considering expelling all free blacks from Britain.

ESSAY QUESTION: *Have you ever tricked someone into murdering his spouse? If so, why are you admitting it?*

PERICLES *(1607) Comedy/Romance*

Setting: Tyre, Antioch, Tarsus, and Pentapolis

Source: *Confessio Amantis* by John Gower.

Best Known For: Being produced only rarely.

Major Characters:

Pericles—Prince of Tyre

Antiochus—King of Antioch

Thaisa—Pericles's wife, eventually

Marina—Their daughter

Plot: Pericles solves a riddle and discovers that Antiochus is having an incestuous affair with his own daughter. Antiochus decides to kill Pericles, who takes off for Tarsus, where he becomes a hero. Then he leaves for Pentapolis and gets in a (surprise, surprise!) shipwreck, but eventually arrives in Pentapolis, where he wins the hand of Thaisa.

Now he receives word that Antiochus has died and that everyone in Tyre wants Pericles to come back. So the newlyweds sail for Tyre and Thaisa has a baby en route, but there's also bad news—it looks as if Thaisa has died during childbirth. Of course, she's alive, but nobody notices and they seal her up in a coffin and throw it into the sea. She eventually washes up on shore and becomes a nun, religious vocations being popular jobs for Shakespearean characters. In the meantime, Pericles leaves their baby daughter to be raised by Dionyza who, sixteen years later, becomes jealous and decides to have her killed. This being a comedy, the daughter is not killed, but Pericles comes across her tomb and is really bummed out. Then he runs into her and is really happy and then finds Thaisa, and they all live happily ever after.

One-Sentence Plot Encapsulation: Pericles fails to win Father of the Year.

Moral: Don't ask someone to solve a riddle whose answer will reveal that you are committing incest.

Famous Quotes:

"Murder's as near to lust as flame to smoke." Act I, Scene 1

"'Tis time to fear when tyrants seem to kiss." Act I, Scene 2

(Okay, they're not famous. But they should be.)

Best Feature: Thaisa's watertight coffin.

Worst Feature: No truly authentic text of this play exists. Some guy named George Wilkins is thought to have written the first half of the play, with Shakespeare writing the second half. Shakespeare should have saved his time.

Rating: 💀💀

Interesting Fact: In Britain, the spelling of a car "tire" is "tyre."

ESSAY QUESTION: *Why do we pay someone to rotate our tires? Don't they rotate on their own?*

RICHARD II (1594) *History*

> **Setting:** England, about 1398
>
> **Source:** Holinshed's *Chronicles* and Hall's *Union*.

Best Known For: Its lyrical poetry and poignant depiction of Richard II's downfall. This play is also the first of four plays (*Richard II; Henry IV, Parts I* and *II*; and *Henry V*) known as the Henriad. The Henriad covers the history of the English crown from 1397 to 1415.

Major Characters:

Richard II—King of England

Henry Bolingbroke—Who will become King Henry IV

Plot: Richard II has been aloof, wasteful, and unwise. He has filled the royal court with his cronies, overtaxed the wealthy, and gotten involved in unpopular wars. Henry Bolingbroke in particular is angry because Richard II has stolen lands that were his due. While Richard II is in Ireland, Bolingbroke takes back his land and the people rally behind him. Richard II is forced to abdicate. Richard II is locked up in Flint Castle, where he is murdered. Bolingbroke, now King Henry IV, vows to begin a crusade to the Holy Land to atone for Richard II's murder.

One-Sentence Plot Encapsulation: Richard proves the old adage: Absolute power corrupts two in the bush.

Moral: Read my lips: No new taxes.

Famous Quotes: "This royal throne of kings, this sceptred isle… This blessed plot, this earth, this realm, this England." Act II, Scene 1

"For God's sake let us sit upon the ground / And tell sad stories of the death of Kings . . ." Act III, Scene 2

Best Feature: Some of Shakespeare's greatest speeches.

Worst Feature: Very talky.

Rating: 💀 💀 💀

Interesting Fact: Some scholars believe Richard II was gay.

FUN FACT: Richard Thomas, John-Boy from *The Waltons*, performed a much-lauded version of *Richard II* at the Shakespeare Theatre in Washington, D.C.

ESSAY QUESTION: *Is it okay to overthrow a king if he's gay? If so, why?*

RICHARD III (1592) *History*

Setting: England, beginning in 1477

Source: Holinshed's *Chronicles* and Hall's *Union.*

Best known for: The title character, King Richard III, the evil hunchback. This is the first great play that Shakespeare wrote.

Major Characters:

Richard Plantagenet—Later, King Richard III

The Duke of Buckingham—Richard's right-hand man

The Duke of Richmond

Plot: Richard wants to be king. He manipulates and kills people left and right to get his way. He gains the crown, betrays Buckingham, then is killed in battle by the Duke of Richmond.

One-Sentence Plot Encapsulation: The ends justify the means.

Fig. 13. David Garrick as Richard III indicates the sum of 2+3.

Moral: What goes around comes around.

Famous Quote: "A horse! A horse! My kingdom for a horse!" Act V, Scene 4

Best Feature: Richard III is one of the great dramatic villains of all time. He is smart and sexy, as well as violent and evil. In the character of Richard III, we see for the first time one of Shakespeare's greatest traits: the ability to show two sides to every coin.

Worst Feature: The hump on Richard's back is his worst physical feature.

Rating: 🎭 🎭 🎭 🎭

Interesting Fact: There is some evidence that Richard III was known as Humpty because of his humpback. And, believe it or not, the nursery rhyme Humpty Dumpty is allegedly based on the story of Richard III's downfall. Really.

ESSAY QUESTION: *In today's politically correct world, could a playwright portray a physically disabled person in as unsympathetic manner as Shakespeare portrays Richard III? Why not?*

Unconventional Wisdom

The Conventional Wisdom: Shakespeare stole the ideas for his plays from other sources.

The Reduced Wisdom: Shakespeare simply *borrowed* the ideas for his plays from other sources and later returned them to their original owners.

ROMEO AND JULIET *(1594–5) Tragedy*

Setting: Verona

Source: Arthur Brooke's poem from 1562, *The Tragicall History of Romeus and Juliet, itself* based on the work of Giraldi Cinthio. And the musical *West Side Story*; Shakespeare removed the music and changed the setting from New York to Italy.

Best Known For: The sexy romance between the young title characters. Teenagers love this play. (Maybe that's an overstatement. Let's say they like it a little more than most of Shakespeare's other plays.)

Major Characters:

Romeo

Juliet

Friar Laurence

Plot: Romeo falls in love with Juliet, but their families have a longstanding feud, so their love must be kept secret. They get married. Romeo accidentally kills Juliet's cousin and is banished. Juliet's parents, not knowing she is already married, arrange for her to marry a nobleman. Friar Laurence gives Juliet a potion that will make it look like she died right before her wedding to the nobleman. The plan is for Romeo to return after Juliet awakes from her sleep so that they will run away together. But Romeo never receives word of this plan. When he arrives, he is devastated to find Juliet seemingly dead, and he kills himself. Juliet awakens to find Romeo dead. She kills herself, too.

One-Sentence Plot Encapsulation: Shakespeare said it himself in the prologue: "A pair of star-crossed lovers take their life."

Moral: Teen marriages never last.

Famous Quotes:

"Parting is such sweet sorrow." Act II, Scene 2

"What's in a name? That which we call a rose / By any other word would smell as sweet." Act II, Scene 2

"Romeo, Romeo! Wherefore art thou Romeo?" Act II, Scene 2

"A plague o' both your houses." Act III, Scene 1

Best Feature: The play is sexy, delightful, and moving.

Worst Feature: The prologue gives away the ending. There's a reason we don't learn that Darth Vader is Luke's father until the end. Oops! We just gave it away.

Rating: 🎭🎭🎭🎭🎭

Interesting Fact: *Romeo and Juliet* is probably only the second tragedy that Shakespeare wrote.

> **ESSAY QUESTION:** *Shakespeare's tragedies are depressing. Why didn't he write some upbeat tragedies?*

THE TAMING OF THE SHREW (1590–1) *Comedy*

Setting: Italy

Source: The folktale "A Merry Jest of a Shrewde Curste Wife."

Best Known For: Its political incorrectness. It's the story of a man who breaks the will of a strong-minded woman so that she will be a subservient wife. Feminists love it.

Major Characters:

Petruccio—A witty, self-assured man

Kate—An independent, strong-minded woman

Plot: Petruccio wants to marry Kate for her large dowery. Kate's father agrees to the match. Kate has no say in the matter. She is shrewish to Petruccio, but he claims to find her behavior charming. He charmingly refuses her food and sleep until he breaks her spirit. And they live happily ever after.

One-Sentence Plot Encapsulation: Petruccio tames Kate, and vice versa.

Moral: No means yes.

Famous Quotes:

"I'll not budge an inch." Introduction, Scene 1

Katherine: "Asses are made to bear and so are you."

Petruccio: "Women are made to bear and so are you." Act II, Scene 1

"Kiss me, Kate." Act II, Scene 7

Best Feature: Domestic abuse.

Worst Feature: Domestic abuse.

Rating: 🎭🎭🎭

Interesting Fact: Shakespeare spent most of his adult life living in London while his wife and children lived in Stratford.

ESSAY QUESTION: *Some scholars argue that Kate's speech about submission near the end of the play is meant to be ironic. In how many ways are they in denial?*

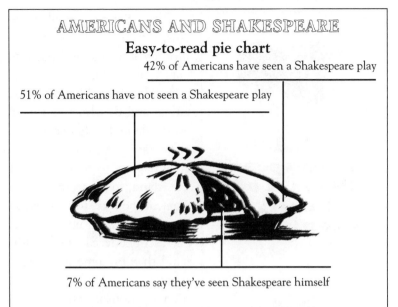

AMERICANS AND SHAKESPEARE
Easy-to-read pie chart
42% of Americans have seen a Shakespeare play

51% of Americans have not seen a Shakespeare play

7% of Americans say they've seen Shakespeare himself

THE TEMPEST (1611) Comedy/Romance

Setting: A tropical island

Source: This play was likely inspired by reports of an actual incident in 1609 when several ships headed to the Virginia Colony. A terrible storm caused a number of vessels to become separated from the rest. One of the ships ran aground in Bermuda, where the crew took nine months to rebuild the vessel before sailing on to Virginia. When this story reached England, it caused a sensation.

Best Known For: Probably being the last play Shakespeare wrote entirely on his own. It is one of his best comedies.

Major Characters:

Prospero—A magician and duke of Milan

Miranda—His daughter

Ariel—A spirit controlled by Prospero

Antonio—Prospero's brother, who usurped his dukedom

Alonso—King of Naples and friend of Antonio

Ferdinand—Son of Alonso

Caliban—Prospero's slave, half-human and half-animal

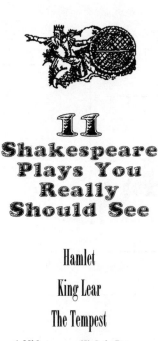

11
Shakespeare Plays You Really Should See

Hamlet

King Lear

The Tempest

A Midsummer Night's Dream

The Lion King

Romeo and Juliet

Macbeth

Henry IV, Part 1

Henry V

Richard III

A Chorus Line

Plot: Before the play begins, Antonio has taken over Prospero's throne and put him out to sea, along with Prospero's daughter, Miranda. The father and daughter ended up on an island. By chance, twelve years later, Antonio and his crew happen to be sailing past the island, so Prospero uses his magical powers to shipwreck them. They wash up on shore, but as nobody can find Ferdinand they presume he is dead. Antonio plots to kill his good friend, Alonso, while Ferdinand falls in love with Miranda. Other members of the shipwrecked crew plot with Caliban to kill Prospero. Ariel is able to let Prospero know everything that's going on. Finally, Prospero reveals himself to his brother and demands back his throne. They learn that Ferdinand is alive and about to marry Miranda. His royal power restored, Prospero gives up his magic and frees Ariel and Caliban.

One-Sentence Plot Encapsulation: Prospero discovers that not even stranding his daughter on an island will keep her from discovering boys.

Moral: If you're going to take over your brother's kingdom, don't set him adrift at sea. Kill him instead.

Famous Quotes:

"Misery acquaints a man with strange bedfellows." Act II, Scene 2

"We are such stuff / As dreams are made on . . ."Act IV, Scene 1

"O brave new world, That has such people in't!" Act V, Scene 1

Best Feature: The play feels like Shakespeare's valediction.

Worst Feature: Another shipwreck (although, to be fair, it was based on an actual incident).

Rating:

Interesting Fact: Many see the character of Prospero as the embodiment of Shakespeare himself on the verge of retirement. As such, when Prospero lays down his magic book and breaks his stick, it is thought of as Shakespeare's farewell before returning to Stratford.

11 Plays That Are Hard to Sit Through

Titus Andronicus

Troilus and Cressida

Timon of Athens

Nicholas Nickleby

Coriolanus

King John

Henry VI, Part Whichever

Henry VIII

Angels in America, Parts 1 & 2

ESSAY QUESTION: *If you rearrange the letters in the name Caliban, it almost spells "cannibal." Have you seen* Silence of the Lambs?

TIMON OF ATHENS (1605) *Tragedy*

Setting: You guessed it: Athens!

Source: Plutarch's *Lives*.

Best Known For: The extreme character of Timon. He is overly generous until he runs out of money. And then he curses humanity for the rest of the play.

Major Characters:

Timon of Athens

Plot: Timon tries to buy popularity with his wealth. Then he runs out of money and nobody will help him. Timon becomes a hermit. He digs for food, but finds gold instead. All his "friends" now come calling again, looking for a handout. Some senators come to visit, ostensibly to apologize for the way they have treated Timon, but really to ask for money. He refuses them, writes his own epitaph, and kicks the bucket.

One-Sentence Plot Encapsulation: Shakespeare did it better in a little rewrite he called *King Lear*.

Moral: A fool and his money are soon parted.

Famous Quote:

"Can't buy me love." It's not from *Timon of Athens*, but the sentiment's right.

Best Feature: Hmm. That's a tough one.

Worst Feature: This is Shakespeare's most mind-numbingly pessimistic play.

Rating: 💀

Interesting Fact: Some scholars believe that Shakespeare co-wrote this play with Thomas Middleton. Others believe that this play was never completed, as there is no record of it having been performed during Shakespeare's lifetime, and the version that exists is only a rough draft. In other words, this play stinks.

ESSAY QUESTION: *Have you ever seen* Phantom of the Opera? *Is it possible that Andrew Lloyd Webber co-wrote it with Thomas Middleton?*

TITUS ANDRONICUS (1593) *Tragedy*

Sources: Plutarch's *Lives*, Euripides's *Hecuba*, Ovid's *Metamorphoses*, and Seneca's *Thyestes*.

Setting: Ancient Rome

Best Known For: Being Shakespeare's first tragedy and the bloodiest play he wrote. It's an Elizabethan slasher drama.

Major Characters:

Titus Andronicus—Roman general

Lavinia—His daughter

Saturninus—The Roman emperor

Bassianus—His younger brother and the love of Lavinia

Tamora—Queen of the Goths, lover of Saturninus

Chiron and Demetrius—Sons of Tamora

Aaron—Lover of Tamora

Plot: It's an Elizabethan revenge tragedy. As such, it foreshadows much better plays to come, such as *Hamlet*, *King Lear*, and *Sweeney Todd*. Chiron and Demetrius encounter Saturninus and Lavinia in the woods. They murder Saturninus and rape Lavinia, then cut out her tongue and chop off her hands so that she cannot tell anyone who's responsible for what happened. Aaron frames Titus's sons for Saturninus's murder and tells Titus that the emperor will spare their lives if Titus will cut off his own hand and send it to him. Titus does so, but his sons are killed anyway. Lavinia communicates to Titus that Chiron and Demetrius are responsible for her condition, so Titus kills them and then serves them in a pie to Tamora and Saturninus at dinner. Titus kills Lavinia to end her suffering, then kills Tamora. Saturninus kills Titus and is then killed himself.

One-Sentence Plot Encapsulation: Groundlings love blood!

Moral: Payback is hell.

Famous Quote:

"Jesus! Look at all the blood!" (Not said in the play itself, but by audiences in the theater. Also by everyone who saw Mel Gibson's *The Passion of the Christ*.)

Best Feature: Rapist pie.

Worst Feature: Ten murders in Act II alone.

Rating: 🎭🎭🎭

Interesting Fact: Although one of Shakespeare's most popular plays in his day, it's rarely performed today. He probably co-wrote it with George Peele.

ESSAY QUESTION: *T. S. Eliot said that* Titus Andronicus *is ". . . one of the stupidest and most uninspiring plays ever written." Discuss.*

TROILUS AND CRESSIDA *(1602) Comedy/Problem Play*

Setting: The Trojan War, about 1193 BC

Source: Homer's *The Iliad*, and Chaucer's *Troilus and Criseyde*.

Best Known For: Nothing.

Major Characters:

Troilus—Youngest son of the king of Troy

Hector—Troilus's older brother

Cressida—A beautiful Trojan woman, lover of Troilus

Pandarus—Cressida's uncle

Diomedes—A Greek commander

Achilles—The greatest Greek soldier

Patroclus—Achilles's best friend, and maybe his lover

Plot: In the seventh year of the Trojan War, Hector issues a challenge to fight any Greek soldier. In the midst of all this, Troilus falls in love with the beautiful Cressida. She says she loves him, too, but when she is exchanged for a prisoner, she flirts with the Greek commanders. She falls for Diomedes and gives him a love token that Troilus had given her. Troilus sees this and swears to slay Diomedes. The next day in battle, Hector slays Patroclus. Achilles is so angry that he has his men kill Hector. Troilus curses Achilles for killing his brother.

One-Sentence Plot Encapsulation: Trojan Wars are complicated.

Moral: Trojans sometimes break . . . your heart.

Famous Quote: Nope.

Best Feature: The play is very modern in that it attacks everything and everyone and seems to have no moral certainties.

Worst Feature: You name it: lots of unsympathetic characters. Lots of references to Greek and Roman mythology that today's audiences don't understand. Plus, the tone is very pessimistic and the structure is disjointed. Other than that, it's a great play.

Rating: 🎭

Interesting Fact: George Bernard Shaw considered this play a masterpiece. He is alone in that assessment.

> **ESSAY QUESTION:** *Was one of your siblings considered the family's "problem child"? Did they get this label simply because they were not as funny as they should have been?*

TWELFTH NIGHT *(1601) Comedy*
Setting: Greece
Source: *Gl' Ingannati*, an Italian comedy published in 1537.
Best Known For: Malvolio, a truly funny character who takes himself far too seriously.
Major Characters:
Count Orsino—A nobleman
Viola—A young lady
Sebastian—Her twin brother
Olivia—A rich countess
Malvolio—Olivia's steward
Sir Toby Belch—Olivia's uncle
Plot: Viola and her twin brother are shipwrecked and separated off the coast of Illyria. Viola disguises herself as a boy and becomes a page to Orsino, with whom she falls in love. But Orsino is in love with Olivia, who will not be wooed because she is in mourning. Nonetheless, she falls in love with Orsino's page the moment she lays eyes upon him. Meanwhile, Sir Toby and Malvolio have a disagreement. Malvolio is tricked into thinking that Olivia is in love with him by Sir Toby, who wants revenge. He convinces Malvolio to dress and act strangely in order to approach Olivia. Malvolio is pronounced crazy and locked away. Now Olivia runs into Viola's twin brother, Sebastian, mistakes him for the page she is in love with, and they agree to marry. Eventually, Sebastian meets up with Viola and they recognize each other. No longer having to pretend to be a boy, she and Orsino fall in love. The only one who ends up unhappy is Malvolio, who promises revenge on them all.

One-Sentence Plot Encapsulation: Transvestism leads to love.

Moral: Threesomes are complicated.

Famous Quotes:

"If music be the food of love, play on." Act I, Scene 1

"Some are born great, some achieve greatness, and some have greatness thrust upon 'em." Act II, Scene 4

Best Feature: Considered one of Shakespeare's greatest comedies, along with *Much Ado About Nothing*, *As You Like It*, and *A Midsummer Night's Dream*.

Worst Feature(s): Shipwreck. Cross-dressing. Character A in love with Character B who loves Character C. We've seen it before.

Rating: 💀💀💀💀.

Interesting Fact: In Shakespeare's day, the holiday called "Twelfth Night" was January 6, the last day of the Christmas season. On this day, they celebrated the Feast of the Epiphany. People played practical jokes on each other and the normal rules of society were suspended.

ESSAY QUESTION: *In Shakespeare's day, the women's roles were played by boys. So for the part of Viola, a boy would have been playing a girl playing a boy. Explain this. Please.*

Two Gentlemen of Verona (1590–1) *Comedy*

Setting: Italy

Source: *Diana Enamorada* by Jorge de Montemayor.

Best Known For: Its inaccurate geographic references. And its inexplicable ending. And, of course, for cross-dressing. It was probably Shakespeare's first play.

Major Characters:

Valentine—One of the titular gentlemen of Verona

Proteus—The other titular gentleman of Verona

Sylvia—Daughter of the duke of Milan

Julia—Proteus's love

Launce—Proteus's comic servant

Plot: Good friends Valentine and Proteus both fall in love with Sylvia. Comic hijinks ensue. Valentine marries Sylvia. Proteus marries Julia.

One-Sentence Plot Encapsulation: Combine the first two sentences of the plot description above into a single sentence.

Moral: Threesomes are complicated.

Best Feature: The servant character Launce and his pet dog, Crab, are very funny. They usually steal the show.

Famous Quote: None. The dog doesn't have any lines.

Worst Feature: In the final scene, Proteus, who has nearly raped Sylvia, is hardly sorry for his actions and immediately falls back in love with Julia when her identity is revealed. And even though his friend, Valentine, is in love with Sylvia, he doesn't think twice about forgiving Proteus. It's all pretty slapdash. That said, there are still a lot of laughs in the play.

Rating: Three Bards

Interesting Fact: In Shakespeare's day, parents often arranged marriages between people who hardly knew each other. Today, reality television producers often arrange marriages between people who hardly know each other.

ESSAY QUESTION: W. C. Fields said never to work with animals or kids. Discuss.

TWO NOBLE KINSMEN *(1613–4) Comedy/Romance*

Setting: Ancient Greece

Source: Chaucer's *Knight's Tale* and Boccaccio's *Teseide.*

Best Known For: Being only partially written by Shakespeare. Scholars believe that John Fletcher wrote about half of it. It is believed to be Shakespeare's last play.

Major Characters:

Palamon—Nephew of the King of Thebes, cousin of Arcite

Arcite—Nephew of the King of Thebes, cousin of Palamon

Theseus—Duke of Athens

Emilia—Sister of Theseus, loved by both Palamon and Arcite

Plot: Palamon and Arcite are cousins, soldiers, and best friends. They are captured while fighting the Athenians. While in prison they both fall for Emilia and compete for her love, which doesn't do much for their friendship. As Theseus doesn't like what's going on, he exiles Arcite, while leaving Palamon in the slammer. But the jailer's daughter has the hots for Palamon and helps him escape from prison (she later goes mad when she realizes Palamon does not love her). Once out, Palamon meets up with Arcite. They are about to fight to settle their dispute over Emilia, when that pesky Theseus finds them and orders that they be killed. Emilia pleads on behalf of the cousins, so Theseus banishes them instead. One problem—they refuse to go. Theseus tells Emilia to pick one man, and he'll have the other killed. She can't do it, so it's decided they will duel after all; the winner will marry Emilia, and the loser will die. The long-awaited duel finally happens and Arcite wins, but before Palamon can be executed, Arcite is thrown from a horse and dies—but not before telling his cousin to marry Emilia.

One-Sentence Plot Encapsulation: Boys meet girl, boys lose girl, boy gets girl but dies, so *other* boy gets girl.

Moral: Don't fall in love with the same girl as your best friend.

Famous Quote: None.

Best Feature: It's an interesting examination of the conflict between love and friendship.

Worst Feature: The characters Palamon and Arcite are too similar.

Rating: 🖋

Interesting Fact: The madness of the jailer's daughter seems to be a reprise of Ophelia in *Hamlet*.

ESSAY QUESTION: *Why is most of Act I of* Two Noble Kinsmen *irrelevant to the main plot? Extra credit: Since almost no one has ever seen this play, does the irrelevance of Act I matter?*

THE WINTER'S TALE (1610–1) *Comedy/Romance*
  Setting: Bulimia; sorry, Bohemia
  Source: Robert Greene's *Pandosto.*

Best Known For: Its mood shifting 180 degrees from the jealousy and vengefulness at the beginning to forgiveness and redemption at the end. Audiences have trouble accepting some of the play's absurdities.

Major Characters:

Leontes—King of Sicilia

Polixenes—King of Bohemia and friend of Leontes

Hermione—Leontes's queen

Perdita—Leontes's and Hermione's daughter

Florizel—Polixenes's son

Plot: Ready for this? Polixenes is visiting Leontes and wants to go home. Leontes asks Hermione to convince Polixenes to stay. She does, but because she is so persuasive, Leontes is convinced they are having an affair. Come on now, Leontes! You asked her to talk to him! Anyway, Leontes decides to kill Polixenes (his best friend), so Polixenes hightails it back to Bohemia. Oh, yes, and Leontes has his wife tried for adultery. While she is in prison, she has a daughter, and Leontes wants the baby killed but is convinced instead to have his man leave the infant in the desert, which he does shortly before being eaten by a bear. Still with us? Okay. Sixteen years pass. Hermione's dead and the kids are grown. All of a sudden, Leontes starts to regret being such a jerk. Too bad he didn't come to that realization earlier, but then there wouldn't be much of a play. Now Florizel (Polixenes's son) and Perdita (Leontes's and Hermione's daughter) fall in love, but Polixenes (Florizel's father) doesn't know that Perdita is of royal blood. He thinks his son has fallen in love with a shepherd girl and isn't happy about it. So the lovers run away to Sicily, followed by Polixenes, who now reconciles with Leontes, and they figure out that the two kids can get married because they're both royalty. The one damper on the whole thing is that Hermione remains dead. But—wait for it—she isn't really dead, she's just been faking it for sixteen years, disguised as a statue. She magically comes back to life, and they all live happily ever after. Give us a break.

One-Sentence Plot Encapsulation: Statues can come back to life.

Moral: It's okay to go nuts and try to kill your wife and your best friend and abandon your infant in the desert—as long as you regret it later.

Famous Quote *and* Best Feature: The best stage direction in the history of drama: "Exit, pursued by a bear."

Worst Feature: A statue coming to life. Oh, come on!

Rating: 💀 💀 💀

Interesting Fact: *The Winter's Tale* was performed by Shakespeare's troupe, the King's Men, as part of the celebration of the wedding of King James I's daughter in 1613.

> **ESSAY QUESTION:** *In this play a baby is abandoned on the shores of Bohemia, a country with no coastline. Make up some smart-ass essay question about that "genius" Shakespeare's knowledge of geography and then answer it.*

Rating the Plays

Let's recap, shall we? Throughout this chapter, we've given each of Shakespeare's plays a rating of one to five Bards, five, of course, being the highest. We've compiled those ratings below for the sake of easy comparison. We did not make these ratings lightly. We researched extensively each play in the canon, taking into account its poetry, themes, relevance, characters, plot, and entertainment value. Then we polled three or four of our friends. And then we just randomly put them in a somewhat haphazard order to stir debate and generate angry letters.

Five Bards 💀 💀 💀 💀 💀

Hamlet
Henry IV, Part 1
King Lear
Macbeth
A Midsummer Night's Dream
Richard III
Romeo and Juliet

Four Bards 💀 💀 💀 💀

As You Like It
Henry V
Julius Caesar
Much Ado About Nothing
Othello
The Tempest
Twelfth Night

Three Bards 💀 💀 💀

The Comedy of Errors
Measure for Measure
Merchant of Venice
The Merry Wives of Windsor
Richard II
The Taming of the Shrew
Two Gentlemen of Verona
The Winter's Tale

Two Bards 💀 💀

All's Well That Ends Well
Antony and Cleopatra
Cymbeline
Henry IV, Part 2
Love's Labour's Lost
Pericles
Titus Andronicus

One Bard 💀

Coriolanus
Henry VI, Parts 1, 2 and 3
Henry VIII
King John
Timon of Athens
Troilus and Cressida
Two Noble Kinsmen

Zero Bards

Cardenio

Most Underrated

(We're not saying they're
great, but maybe there's
more to them than every-
body says.)
Cymbeline
Pericles
Titus Andronicus

Most Overrated

(We're not saying they're
terrible, but maybe they're
not as great as everybody
says.)
As You Like It
The Merchant of Venice
The Winter's Tale

**ESSAY
QUESTION:** Is
Shakespeare's work
relevant today?
Why not?

The Globe
THEATRE

lazzeer-floyd
illuminator

skye box

pea-nut gallery

VIP Lounge
(no champagne)

ringlings

main gallery

female
grouplings

the stage

wurst & ale
vendors

moshe pit

cheap sea

groundlings

ACTING SHAKESPEARE

"Speak the speech, I pray you, as I pronounced it to you,
trippingly on the tongue . . ."
Hamlet, Act III, Scene 2

cademics love to study
Shakespeare, write about
his life and work, debate his
significance, and generally go on and
on about him *ad nauseam*.

But Shakespeare wrote his work to be seen and heard, not
read. His plays were published long after they had been first
performed, as an afterthought. This doesn't mean they don't
make great reading, if you have an excess of free time and not
much of a life. But it does mean that they're best enjoyed seen
live, performed outdoors, under the stars,
huddled under a blanket on a date, after a
couple of bottles of wine, bored to death,
and freezing your butt off.

But how should the works of
Shakespeare be performed today? How
were they performed in his time? Can
people of today understand the language of Shakespeare? Does Shakespeare provide hints within his texts
about how to act them? Could we possibly posit a few more questions?

Fig. 14. The Globe Theatre—actual size. People were smaller in those days.

Acting Shakespeare in His Time

Shakespeare was a popular entertainer—the Wayne Newton of his time, if you will. He wrote plays to please the masses (Shakespeare that is, not Wayne Newton). The plays were long because, although people's life spans were considerably shorter in those days, their attention spans were considerably longer. They expected and demanded that the performances go on . . . and on . . . and on . . . and boy, did they ever. An uncut performance of *Hamlet* could run well over four hours. And for reasons that are now obscure, audiences thought this was great.[43]

In the Elizabethan era, there was a general perception among people who cared about those sorts of things (such as Puritans and censors) that theater was unseemly, that it attracted people of a low moral character, and that it stimulated "whorish lust." Absolutely correct: That was precisely the appeal.

Like a good date, theater was fun and a little naughty. What was not to like? At the theater, one could find gambling, hucksters and hustlers, drinking and eating, and women of ill repute. The whole thing was rather like what goes on today in Washington, D.C. And in the same way that our national leaders today preach moral values while at the same time embezzling, womanizing, and funneling government money to their cronies, in Shakespeare's day, members of the royalty loved the theater while still allowing their lower-level bureaucrats to shut it down from time to time.

Unlike today, in Shakespeare's time there was a minority of self-righteous busybodies who deemed it their job to control what everyone else did. They weren't content to simply live their own lives in a "moral" manner and leave the rest of the populace alone. Instead, they believed it was their God-given duty to make everyone else live the same repressed way they did. On more than

---

[43] As always, though, there is contradictory evidence on this point. Some believe that in Shakespeare's day, performances typically lasted only two hours because the actors zipped through their lines at breakneck speed. Really. In which case the Reduced Shakespeare Company's fast, funny, and physical performances are far more Shakespearean in spirit than we previously imagined.

one occasion, these people actually succeeded in shutting down all the theaters in London on moral grounds. Fortunately, this sort of thing would never happen today. Thank goodness, people like that aren't around anymore.

An interesting effect of the generally low moral standing of theater in the sixteenth century was that women were not allowed to be actors. To be an actress was considered tantamount to being a prostitute. At the same time, Shakespeare was writing great female roles in his plays. The dilemma was obvious.

With no female actors, who would play the women in the plays—Juliet, Ophelia, Lady Macbeth? The answer was simple: Young boys played the female roles. (It was said that actor Thomas Pope's performance as Cleopatra was particularly fetching, and that he subsequently had to fight off male admirers.) These lads donned wigs, makeup, dresses, and minced around the stage portraying the love interests of older male actors. For some reason, this practice was considered perfectly acceptable.

Despite all this moral concern, in those days there were government subsidies for the arts. The Lord Chamberlain, and later King James himself, sponsored Shakespeare's company of actors.

Shakespeare's Actors

Scholars believe that during his professional life, Shakespeare was a member of only a few acting companies. It's believed (though there's no evidence) that he performed with Lord Leicester's Men, then joined Lord Strange's Men—which sounds like the title of a dirty movie, but was really just an acting company. Shakespeare later joined the Lord Chamberlain's Men, who later became known as the King's Men. (All of these companies were named after their royal patrons.) Early in his career, Shakespeare is known to have acted in plays by authors other than himself, which is probably where he first developed the notion that he could write better plays than hacks like Ben Jonson.

Shakespeare knew his fellow actors well: their strengths, their weaknesses, their party tricks, and their bad habits. He probably wrote most of his greatest roles for specific actors he knew would play them. (You can't write a role as great as Juliet unless you've got just the right boy to play her.) And, in another measure of the man's genius, he used this knowledge of his company's skills to create compelling dramatic characters that hadn't been seen onstage before.

One example is Shakespeare's transformation of the "Vice," an archetypal character familiar to Elizabethan audiences. The Vice was a character from medieval morality plays, a shrunken, ugly, troublemaking clown who provided comic relief while subverting the order of the play (and often order in general). Shakespeare had several great clowns in his company (Will Kemp and Robert Armin, among others), and from his own experience playing old men, knew that actors chafe under the limitations of playing only one kind of role. His inspired idea was to *combine* roles—to transform the Vice into a leading character, and *voilà!* We have the shrunken, ugly, troublemaking Richard III. A level of wit, as well as a comic rapport with the audience, turned what could have been a one-dimensional villain into a compelling and almost endearing-in-spite-of-his-actions creation.

The same might be said for Shylock. What had been a one-dimensional, anti-Semitic caricature in Marlowe's *The Jew of Malta* becomes a complete and rounded character in *The Merchant of Venice,* when Shakespeare imbues him with humanity (while at the same time allowing his actors to bring their full arsenal of tricks to the creation of the character). And Iago—this leading role might well have been originally played by a supporting actor who was able to bring his own professional jealousies and spite to the role. This was only possible because the actors had a playwright as a member of their company, one who was a former actor who could write to their strengths.

Peter Thomson, in *Shakespeare's Professional Career,* says "that Shakespeare empowered his actors as no English playwright had done before him." True, but not completely, and not at the expense of the story. He probably disdained improvisation, if Hamlet's advice to the players is any reflection of Shakespeare's own feelings:

> . . . And let those that play your clowns speak no more than is set down for them—for there be of them that will them-

selves laugh, to set on some quantity of barren spectators to laugh, too, though in the meantime some necessary question of the play be then to be considered. (Act III, Scene 2)

Shakespeare appears to be speaking with the voice of experience. Will Kemp tended to go off the script and incorporate some of the legendary dancing for which he was famous, but which Shakespeare justifiably thought took away from the story at hand.

Elizabethan Acting

How was the style of a Shakespearean performance different then from now? This question is almost impossible to answer because almost no movies exist of Shakespearean performances from Shakespeare's time. But one imagines that the style of delivery must be similar: strong, loud voices to reach the back of a large theater, overarticulation for clarity of speech, and large, exaggerated movements to portray the emotional extremes so common in Shakespeare's work. In other words: bad acting then, bad acting now. Even the oldest existing sound recordings we have of Shakespearean performances, which date back only about one hundred years, sound phony and sing-songy to the modern ear. With the advent of television and film, audiences have come to expect a more naturalistic style of acting. Why most Shakespearean actors today choose to confound that expectation remains a mystery.

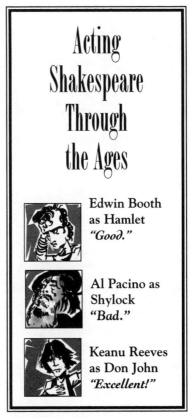

Acting Shakespeare Through the Ages

Edwin Booth as Hamlet *"Good."*

Al Pacino as Shylock *"Bad."*

Keanu Reeves as Don John *"Excellent!"*

Shakespeare's Actors

The First Folio lists "The Names of the Principall Actors in all thefe Playes," but fist-fights still break out when scholars debate which actor originally played which Shakespearean role. Here's an easy-to-follow chart, explaining at a glance who these master thespians were, along with our best guesses as to which roles they might have played (as well as their equivalent in today's celebrity currency).

ACTOR	ROLES PROBABLY PLAYED	CHARACTER TYPE	CONTEMPORARY COUNTERPART
William Shakespeare	The Ghost and Polonius in *Hamlet,* Theseus in *Midsummer Night's Dream,* Egeon in *Comedy of Errors,* King Henry in *Henry IV, Part 1*	Playwright/actor, played small roles, mostly weird old men	Playwright/actor and small, weird old man — **Woody Allen**
Richard Burbage	Hamlet, Lear, Othello	Leading man famous for Tragedies	Leading man **Kevin Spacey**, famous for Tragedies like *The Life of David Gale* and *K-PAX*
Will Kemp	Dogberry in *Much Ado About Nothing,* Falstaff in *Henry IV, Part 1*	Clown, specialized in funny dancing	Sweathog clown **John Travolta**, who danced funny in *Saturday Night Fever* and *Pulp Fiction*
John Hemminges	Falstaff in *Merry Wives of Windsor*	Actor who got more credit than he deserved for co-editing First Folio	Actor who got more credit than he deserved for writing *Good Will Hunting*—**Matt Damon**
Henry Condell	Unknown	Actor who got more credit than he deserved for co-editing First Folio	Actor who got more credit than he deserved for writing *Good Will Hunting*—**Ben Affleck**
Nathan Field	Bernardo in *Hamlet* Macbeth in *Macbeth*	Child actor, played characters who see ghosts	Dead people–seeing **Haley Joel Osment**
John Sinkloe	Slender in *Merry Wives of Windsor,* Aguecheek, *Twelfth Night*	Vapid nonentity who moved from monosyllabic supporting roles to monosyllabic leading roles	**Keanu Reeves**
Samuel Gilburne	Viola, *Twelfth Night*	Androgynous actor, played women playing men; won Olden Globe award	Androgynous man–playing, Golden Globe–winner **Hilary Swank.**

Interestingly, scholars believe that the English accent of the sixteenth century was not like the English accent of today. In fact, there is evidence that Elizabethan English sounded much like American English does today. This means that Kenneth Branagh may not be our most authentic Shakespearean actor, but rather Keanu Reeves.

Acting Shakespeare Today

Today, much about the theater is different from the way it was in Shakespeare's time. Women are allowed to perform onstage. And young male actors do not have to dress up as women, except for their own enjoyment. The acting profession is considered completely legitimate and is held in the same esteem as a lawyer or a politician or a professional athlete. (Maybe those are bad examples.) Let's just say that today actors are not considered the equivalent of prostitutes. Well, not quite.

Are the Shakespeare plays we see performed today all that different from the way they were performed in his day? Good question. In many ways the experience would be similar: The casts are still generally large, props are usually minimal, and costumes are frequently lavish.

In other ways, though, contemporary productions are different. Many are performed at night. This was not possible in the sixteenth century because neither electricity nor professional baby-sitting services yet existed. All performances were matinees. And in Shakespeare's time there were no Shakespeare festivals. Nor were there intermissions, bathrooms in the theater, or school matinees. Also, Shakespeare was not yet on academic curricula, to the delight of millions of Elizabethan-era schoolchildren.

Style

In Shakespeare's time, the playwright would write the script and the actors would rehearse the show by themselves, as written. It was a straightforward process that was true to the playwright's vision. Today, it's more complicated because a theater director oversees the entire process, determining the overall artistic vision of the production, including what time period in which to set the

WHY IS SHAKESPEARE SO POPULAR?

Why do so many companies perform Shakespeare today?
Is it because of his timeless themes? Is it because he profoundly understood the human condition?

No.

It's because Shakespeare has been dead for so long that his works are in the public domain. Hence, producers do not have to pay a solitary penny in royalties when mounting his plays.

production, the music, the lighting— in effect, the entire style of the piece. In the old days, they would put on the show as written, in the time and place that Shakespeare described. Today, it is the job of the director to make the play as different from what Shakespeare intended as is humanly possible while still mostly using Shakespeare's actual words.

All of this futzing by a director is done under the pretext of making the play accessible or relevant to a modern audience, as if that were really possible. People today have much shorter attention spans than people did in Elizabethan times. No one is certain why this is the case. Some experts believe it is the influence of television and the Internet. Others blame Satan. But no matter the cause, most directors now cut large sections from Shakespeare's plays in order to shorten them to suit the tastes of today's audiences.

In an odd twist, however, almost all productions of Shakespeare today have an intermission or two during the performance, each of which adds fifteen or twenty minutes to the length of the show. The audience uses this time to get a strong cup of coffee in the hope of staying awake during the next act.

In Shakespeare's day, there were no intermissions. The show ran from beginning to end without stop. Vendors sold beer, water, oranges, nuts, gingerbread, and apples to throw at the actors. From time to time, patrons would actually consume these things instead of flinging them. Audience members would come and go to stretch their legs or relieve themselves in a ditch outside the theater. They might arrive late and leave early. In short, it was like a

Dodgers game. Except that they didn't sing "Take Me Out to the Ball Game" during the seventh-inning stretch. In those days, they sang "God Save the Queen" during the seventh-inning stretch. Obviously, when Queen Elizabeth I passed away and King James succeeded to the throne, they no longer sang "God Save the Queen." At that point, they changed the song to "The Hokey-Pokey."

Fig. 15. Shakespearean clown Will Kemp prepares to put his right leg in.

Some scholars argue that these many distractions in the theater are the reason that Shakespeare repeated so much information in the text of his plays. If an audience member was out of the theater when something was mentioned the first time, he could hear it later when he came back.

Advice to the Players

Since these plays are meant to be performed, we'd like to provide a few Shakespearean acting tips. The Reduced Shakespeare Company has been acting Shakespeare since 1981. We don't claim to act it well, but we certainly do it frequently. Here are a few valuable tidbits we've learned over the years.

First, if you're auditioning for or cast in a Shakespearean role, read the entire play. This seems like obvious advice, but you'd be surprised how many actors skip this vital step (like us, for instance). By reading the play you'll learn the overall story, as well as what the other characters say about your character when you're offstage.

Speaking the Speech

There's no need to be intimidated by Shakespeare's language.

Although some of the words that Shakespeare used have changed meaning over the last four hundred years and others have fallen into disuse, most of Shakespeare's vocabulary has the same meaning today as when he wrote the plays.

To save you a little time, here are definitions of some words that have fallen out of common usage:

Zounds	God's wounds
Moonish	Fickle
Firk	Strike or beat
Costard	Large apple, also slang for "head"
Liege	A person of higher standing to whom one owes allegiance
Pied	Multicolored
Wherefore	Why
Descry	To see something in the distance, or to investigate

And here are a few words whose meanings have changed since Shakespeare's time:

	Shakespearean Meaning	Today's Meaning
Fond	Foolish	Having affection for
Cool	Slightly cold	Groovy
Hot	Very warm	Sexy
Bad	Not good	Very good
Sweet	Sugary	Very nice
Sup	To feed	What's going on?

If reading the entire play is too much for you, don't despair. We highly recommend a few books that provide short, snappy, and highly readable accounts of Shakespeare's plays: *Stories from Shakespeare* by Marchette Chute, *Tales from Shakespeare* by Charles and Mary Lamb, and *Shakespeare Stories* and *Shakespeare Stories II* by Leon Garfield. These books are also great resources for playgoers. If you read these synopses before seeing one of Shakespeare's plays, it will take you only ten or fifteen minutes, instead of the usual forty, to figure out what's going on.

Second, in acting Shakespeare, always look up any words you don't understand. *A Shakespeare Glossary* by C. T. Onions is a great place to find these definitions (although real Shakespeare nerds insist on using the gigantic *Oxford English Dictionary*). And don't forget that some words that you think you understand, you really don't. Definitions have evolved over time. As Johnny Cochrane might have said, if anyone had bothered to ask him, "When in doubt, check it out." (See page 124.)

Third, you should research any historical or mythological references that occur in Shakespeare. Most of these were common knowledge in Elizabethan times, but today a lot of it can seem obscure.

Fourth, act *on* the lines, not *between* the lines. In other words, the plays are long enough, so don't make them longer by adding pauses in which to emote. Nobody wants an eight-hour production of *Hamlet*. Act and say the words at the same time.

And, finally, understand Shakespeare's verse and respect it, but don't be a slave to it. The rhythmic meter is there as a guidepost, as Shakespeare's way of telling you how to say the lines. Conveying Shakespeare's meaning is more important than getting the beat right. Of course, today's great Shakespearean actors—Ian McKellen, Derek Jacobi, Keanu Reeves—sound natural when they speak and are true to the verse at the same time, but they make it look as easy as breathing. Aye, there's the rub.

Iambic Pentameter

What is iambic pentameter? It's tough to define, but like art or pornography, you know it when you see it. Let's see if we can break it down for you:

There are approximately 104,000 lines in Shakespeare's thirty-seven plays.[44] Of these lines:

  28 percent are in prose
  7 percent are in rhymed verse
  65 percent are in blank verse.

The lines of Shakespeare's blank verse have ten syllables, consisting of five feet of two syllables each. This verse is called Iambic Pentameter.[45]

The iamb is by far the most common metrical foot used by Shakespeare in his blank verse. It has one unaccented and one accented syllable, as in the word "delay." The rhythm of the ten-syllable iambic pentameter line would be duh-DUH duh-DUH duh-DUH duh-DUH duh-DUH, what Ian McKellen calls "the rhythm of the heart."

But there can be variations. Other metrical feet that Shakespeare used are:

Trochee: The opposite of the iambus, in that the first syllable is accented and the second is not, as in "wonder" or "Roman."

Spondee: Two equally stressed syllables. As in "moonbeam" or "heartburn."

Dactyl: A three-syllable foot with the stress on the first syllable. As in "happiness."

Anapest: A three-syllable foot with the stress on the third syllable. As in "unabridged" or "seventeen."

The above information is useful in trying to impress scholarly members of the opposite sex, but apart from that it serves no useful purpose whatsoever.

---

[44] Yes, thirty-seven plays because these statistics exclude *Two Noble Kinsmen*—whose authorship is in some dispute—and *Cardenio*, for which no definitive text exists.

[45] Lines of blank verse in English usually have ten syllables, but not always. For example, if a line has eleven syllables it has what's referred to as a "feminine ending." As Shakespearean scholars, we are always on the lookout for nicely constructed feminine endings.

THE SONNETS AND POETRY OF WILLIAM SHAKESPEARE

"For the sweetest things turn sourest by their deeds;
Lilies that faster smell far worse than weeds."
Sonnet 94

hat do we love about Shakespeare's sonnets? Everything!

• There are only 154 of them.

• They're short: only fourteen lines each, ten syllables per line. No four-hour productions of these babies: you could recite all 154 sonnets in four hours and still have time to go out for pizza.[46]

• With such a strict structure, Shakespeare chose his words carefully. No lengthy soliloquizing here.

• No knowledge of English history required!

• They're about love. Who doesn't like love?

We've talked about Shakespeare's three documented passions (money, social standing, and money). But we can assume that he was also driven to write and stay alive, two impulses that came in very handy during the plague outbreak of 1592. Fifteen thousand people died from the plague that year, and London theaters were closed.[47] Not able to produce

---

[46] If you spoke very quickly and called ahead.

[47] Though actors were guilty of many things, spreading the plague wasn't one of them. But many in authority objected to London's many theaters on both moral and political grounds, and the plague was a good excuse to close them down.

plays, Shakespeare turned to poetry. And not wanting to breathe plague-ridden air, Shakespeare probably moved out of London.

It's possible he went to Stratford, but scholars believe he probably moved in with a prominent patron of the arts named Henry Wriothesley (pronounced, we're not kidding, "Rizley"), who was also the Earl of Southampton. Shakespeare dedicated "Venus and Adonis" and "The Rape of Lucrece" to Southampton for reasons that remain unclear. There are many benign and noble reasons for which Southampton could have encouraged Shakespeare, and for which the young poet could have understandably wanted to offer sincere thanks in his published dedication, but people always want to put the most sordid spin on their relationship. It's outrageous that people always assume there were some naughty, X-rated, extramarital, alternative lifestyle–type things going on between the two men.[48]

However they came to be written, Shakespeare's sonnets are an extraordinary body of work. In Shakespeare's day, sonnet writing was a respectable undertaking: If you wanted to suck up to a patron or a royal, you composed a sonnet. If you wanted to woo a lady, you composed a sonnet. And if you wanted to create a lasting legacy, something that would outlive you and your silly little plays, you composed a sonnet.

That's what Shakespeare did. Written probably between 1592 and 1597, and published in 1609, while he was still alive, Shakespeare's 154 sonnets seem to tell several stories, and they're a biographical treasure trove for scholars who assume Shakespeare was writing journalistic truth and not, you know, fiction.

Analyzing the Sonnets

Whoever wrote, a page ago,[49] that the sonnets are about love doesn't know what the hell he's talking about. If anything, the sonnets are about *death*: how youth can fade, relationships can wither, legacies can disappear, and time can destroy. Thus, the

---

[48] One hates to admit it, but in this case, people are probably right.
[49] It was Austin.

sonnets can be seen as a way to defeat time: to create a body of work that will outlast its creator.

That, at least, is the traditional view. The beauty of the sonnets, however, is that they can be interpreted in literally a billion ways.[50] Like the best of Shakespeare's plays, they depict the paradoxes central to the human experience. They're romantic yet cynical; funny yet serious; specific yet general; worshipful yet dismissive; up yet down; pumpernickel yet whole wheat. They revel in contradiction: "Lilies that fester smell far worse than weeds," Shakespeare observes in Sonnet 94; "In some perfumes is there more delight / Than in the breath that from my mistress reeks," he lovingly declares in Sonnet 130; "Love is my sin, and thy dear virtue hate," he warns in Sonnet 142; and "Am I not love's *bee-yotch?*" he cries in Sonnet 133 (in an admittedly loose paraphrase).

But that's just one view. Here's another: Michael Wood, in his documentary film *In Search of Shakespeare*, speculates that the "Fair Youth" Shakespeare appears to be writing to might very well be his recently deceased son Hamnet. This would explain the pervasive sense of loss in the sonnets, as well as make all those scholars who are uncomfortable with Shakespeare being gay feel a little less icky.

The sonnets are sufficiently rich and varied enough to support any theory you have, but be careful: When reading the sonnets, you must be sure *you've already decided what your theory is.* Do you think Shakespeare was gay? The sonnets support you. Do you think Shakespeare was straight? Sonnet 20 supports that, as well. Do you think Shakespeare was a time-traveler from the future who subsequently returned to his own time, taking all his papers with him? The sonnets prove that, as well (specifically Sonnets 16, 26, 30, 44, 59, and 68 with their references to "Time's pencil," "whatsoever star [i.e., time machine] that guides my moving," "I summon up remembrance of things past [i.e., I set the time coordinates and engage the flux capacitor]," "despite of space I would

---

[50] Mere mortals cannot fully comprehend the actual figure. Not even Stephen Hawking on an espresso bender.

WHO WAS MR. W. H.?

On the title page of the first published edition of the sonnets lies this inscription: "To the onlie begetter of these insuing sonnets Mr. W. H." A begetter, in its old biblical sense, means parent or conceiver. Who was "Mr. W. H.," and in what manner did he nurture or create the sonnets? Did he pay for them? Is he the subject of them? There are many theories, none of them definitive.

Some people actually believe "Mr. W. H." is the previously mentioned Henry Wriothesley, with the initials for some reason reversed. Such is the sorry state of Shakespearean scholarship that this is considered a good guess. These days, the primary candidate—number one with a bullet, as Shakespeare used to say in his old songwriting days—is thought to be a man named William Herbert. It's possible that both Shakespeare and Richard Burbage acted for Herbert's father, the Earl of Pembroke, back in the early 1590s. Shakespeare's friends Hemminges and Condell dedicated the First Folio to Herbert and his brother. And the publisher of the sonnets, Thomas Thorpe, also printed glowing dedications to Herbert in at least two other volumes. Michael Wood, in his book, the imaginatively titled *Shakespeare*, speculates impressively that Herbert might also have been the Fair Youth who so rocked Shakespeare's world, which would explain Herbert as the begetter of the sonnets in the sense of him being their source or inspiration.

But this leads us to the other question: Who made the dedication, Shakespeare or the publisher Thomas Thorpe? This one's pretty easy, actually: The dedication ends with the initials "T. T.," which obviously stand for "Terrific Talent," so it must have been William Shakespeare himself.

be brought / From limits far remote", "your image in some antique book [i.e., which I peruse in some far-off future library]," and "to live a second life" [i.e., my life in the future].

See how easy it is? The sonnets can prove anything!

But remember, and this is important: *never* sit down and read the sonnets without a preconception. *Never* allow the beauty and majesty of Shakespeare's poetry to wash over you and cast its own spell. *Never* approach the sonnets with an open mind. That way madness lies.

Fig. 16. This woodcutting depicts two men who look vaguely Elizabethan.

Understanding the Sonnets

In order to understand the sonnets, you have to take them with several grains of salt. Although today they're numbered 1 through 154, we don't know that Shakespeare assigned those numbers himself. He might have; as they were published during his lifetime, he may have supervised their publication.

We also don't know if they were intended to be read individually, in any order, or in some sort of sequence. Scholars usually divide the sonnets into three categories: Those dealing with "the Fair Youth" with whom Shakespeare was enamored; the ones about "the Rival Poet" with whom he competed; and, of course, "the Dark Lady" after whom he lusted. Don't worry, it's much simpler than that. The sonnets can be easily divided into just two categories: the good sonnets (which are all the ones you've heard of) and the bad (which are all the rest).

POP QUIZ, HOTSHOT
Who was the Dark Lady?

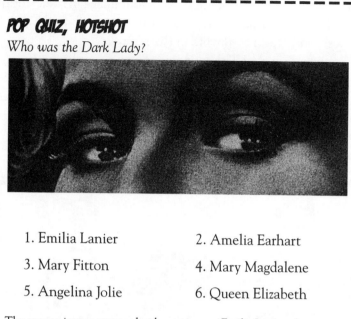

1. Emilia Lanier
2. Amelia Earhart
3. Mary Fitton
4. Mary Magdalene
5. Angelina Jolie
6. Queen Elizabeth

The answer in recent years has been given as Emilia Lanier, the mistress of Lord Hunsdon, the patron of Shakespeare's first company.

A. L. Rowse based this guess on a sixteenth-century document that said "she was very brown in youth," until somebody took another look and saw that it actually said "she was very *brave* in youth." Oops. Mary Fitton was a popular choice until her portrait was discovered; it turns out she was a *blonde*! (Did the carpet match the drapes? History doesn't record.) And Queen Elizabeth, with her hair dyed a fiery red not found in nature and her face pancaked with clown-white makeup, doesn't seem remotely dark, and is actually many people's preferred candidate for the Fair Youth. (Hey, that's no more ridiculous than Angelina Jolie, which was our first guess.)

Unlike his plays, Shakespeare's sonnets were meant to be read. So here are (in our humble opinion) Shakespeare's Top Ten sonnets. Don't worry about the other ones. Read on, Macduff!

ESSAY QUESTION: *Actor, poet, playwright, businessman, philanderer: Is there anything William Shakespeare can't do? Defend yourself.*

The Best of the Sonnets

18.

Shall I compare thee to a summer's day?
Thou art more lovely and more temperate:
Rough winds do shake the darling buds of May,
And summer's lease hath all too short a date:
Sometime too hot the eye of heaven shines,
And often is his gold complexion dimm'd;
And every fair from fair sometime declines,
By chance or nature's changing course untrimm'd;
But thy eternal summer shall not fade
Nor lose possession of that fair thou owest;
Nor shall Death brag thou wander'st in his shade,
When in eternal lines to time thou growest:
  So long as men can breathe or eyes can see,
  So long lives this and this gives life to thee.

29.

When, in disgrace with fortune and men's eyes,
I all alone beweep my outcast state
And trouble deaf heaven with my bootless cries
And look upon myself and curse my fate,
Wishing me like to one more rich in hope,
Featured like him, like him with friends possess'd,
Desiring this man's art and that man's scope,
With what I most enjoy contented least;
Yet in these thoughts myself almost despising,
Haply I think on thee, and then my state,
Like to the lark at break of day arising
From sullen earth, sings hymns at heaven's gate;
  For thy sweet love remember'd such wealth brings
  That then I scorn to change my state with kings.

30.

When to the sessions of sweet silent thought
I summon up remembrance of things past,
I sigh the lack of many a thing I sought,
And with old woes new wail my dear time's waste:
Then can I drown an eye, unused to flow,
For precious friends hid in death's dateless night,
And weep afresh love's long since cancell'd woe,
And moan the expense of many a vanish'd sight:
Then can I grieve at grievances foregone,
And heavily from woe to woe tell o'er
The sad account of fore-bemoaned moan,
Which I new pay as if not paid before.
 But if the while I think on thee, dear friend,
 All losses are restored and sorrows end.

73.

That time of year thou mayst in me behold
When yellow leaves, or none, or few, do hang
Upon those boughs which shake against the cold,
Bare ruin'd choirs, where late the sweet birds sang.
In me thou seest the twilight of such day
As after sunset fadeth in the west,
Which by and by black night doth take away,
Death's second self, that seals up all in rest.
In me thou see'st the glowing of such fire
That on the ashes of his youth doth lie,
As the death-bed whereon it must expire
Consumed with that which it was nourish'd by.
 This thou perceivest, which makes thy love more strong,
 To love that well which thou must leave ere long.

80.

O, how I faint when I of you do write,
Knowing a better spirit doth use your name,
And in the praise thereof spends all his might,
To make me tongue-tied, speaking of your fame!
But since your worth, wide as the ocean is,
The humble as the proudest sail doth bear,
My saucy bark inferior far to his
On your broad main doth wilfully appear.
Your shallowest help will hold me up afloat,
Whilst he upon your soundless deep doth ride;
Or being wreck'd, I am a worthless boat,
He of tall building and of goodly pride:
    Then if he thrive and I be cast away,
    The worst was this; my love was my decay.

91.

Some glory in their birth, some in their skill,
Some in their wealth, some in their bodies' force,
Some in their garments, though new-fangled ill,
Some in their hawks and hounds, some in their horse;
And every humour hath his adjunct pleasure,
Wherein it finds a joy above the rest:
But these particulars are not my measure;
All these I better in one general best.
Thy love is better than high birth to me,
Richer than wealth, prouder than garments' cost,
Of more delight than hawks or horses be;
And having thee, of all men's pride I boast:
    Wretched in this alone, that thou mayst take
    All this away and me most wretched make.

116.

Let me not to the marriage of true minds
Admit impediments. Love is not love
Which alters when it alteration finds,
Or bends with the remover to remove:
O no! it is an ever-fixed mark
That looks on tempests and is never shaken;
It is the star to every wandering bark,
Whose worth's unknown, although his height be taken.
Love's not Time's fool, though rosy lips and cheeks
Within his bending sickle's compass come:
Love alters not with his brief hours and weeks,
But bears it out even to the edge of doom.
   If this be error and upon me proved,
   I never writ, nor no man ever loved.

127.

In the old age black was not counted fair,
Or if it were, it bore not beauty's name;
But now is black beauty's successive heir,
And beauty slander'd with a bastard shame:
For since each hand hath put on nature's power,
Fairing the foul with art's false borrow'd face,
Sweet beauty hath no name, no holy bower,
But is profaned, if not lives in disgrace.
Therefore my mistress' brows are raven black,
Her eyes so suited, and they mourners seem
At such who, not born fair, no beauty lack,
Slandering creation with a false esteem:
   Yet so they mourn, becoming of their woe,
   That every tongue says beauty should look so.

130.

My mistress' eyes are nothing like the sun;
Coral is far more red than her lips' red;
If snow be white, why then her breasts are dun;
If hairs be wires, black wires grow on her head.
I have seen roses damask'd, red and white,
But no such roses see I in her cheeks;
And in some perfumes is there more delight
Than in the breath that from my mistress reeks.
I love to hear her speak, yet well I know
That music hath a far more pleasing sound;
I grant I never saw a goddess go;
My mistress, when she walks, treads on the ground:
*   And yet, by heaven, I think my love as rare*
*   As any she belied with false compare.*

Unconventional Wisdom

The Conventional Wisdom: Shakespeare's sonnets were written to a man with whom Shakespeare was in love.

The Reduced Wisdom: Shakespeare was gay at first, but a church-sponsored program was able to straighten him out.

The Rest of the Sonnets

Our exhaustive research has uncovered four brand-new never-be-fore-seen sonnets by William Shakespeare. Archival experts are poring over them now, but we're 30 percent convinced they're 100 percent authentic, which combines for an overall confidence rating of 65 percent, which we can totally live with.

Shall I compare thee to a dog's dinner?
Thou art more lowly and more desolate:
Rough winds do make a meal, once a winner,
Quite stale and nasty past its sell-by date:
Sometimes too gross the smell of supper seems
And often it is cold leftovers there
And evening fare unfairly often teems

With maggots: signs that owners do not care.
But thy delicious flavor shall not fade
(Can't lose a thing that thou hath never owned)
Nor shall Death on my fear of dying trade
Now I hath from thy close attendance groaned:
    But long as dogs can eat or teeth can chew
    They'll have a shiny coat because of you

Clearly, Shakespeare thought better of offering this inelegant and mildly insulting comparison to his love, and tweaked it ever so slightly to become the Sonnet 18 we know today.

Oh brave new world that hath such people in it!
I'll rattle them off, just give me a minute.
The sprites that fill the air with wondrous lights,
The handsome brave who wears no bulging tights
But steals my breath and calls himself a Man.
Girl, if he can't steal my heart, no one can.
We speak no words, we know not what to say,
I call him Calgon, 'cause he takes me away!
Huzzah, Sir Walter, for arriving here
And bringing home such wondrous weed to smoke—
That England falls and this pristine frontier
Will rise to take its place is okey-doke.
    (Must not forget the man from Nantucket,
    Whose pole was so short he could barely fish with it)

Cut from *The Tempest* in its pre-Broadway tryout. It's atypical rhyme scheme, remarkably prescient political forecasting, and use of twentieth-century urban slang and product placement was deemed too anachronistic for Elizabethan audiences.

Oh dark lady, thou art so aptly named:
You ne'er perceive the glass to be half-full,
To suffer fools you always feel ashamed,
And doth consider cocktail banter bull.
But what to call you, dark lover of mine?

"Late for supper" doth not seem apropos,
And "Gloomy Gert" hath no poetic shine,
Yet one sweet "Highness" and the world would know.
So Dark Lady is what you I shall call
While in this fair affair that we pursue.
Or I could call thee "Queen" and confuse all
'Cause that would fit you, love - and Marlowe too.
I know the glee you feel will be shown never,
Just expressed with a shrug and soft, "whatever"

Found torn apart, burned up, and tossed in the Thames. Historians must now completely rethink Queen Elizabeth I's reign in light of Shakespeare's portrait of her as a kind of Goth Valley Girl.

That time and year thou mayst in me behold
Is far off distant yet and still to come;
That future time when you and yours are cold
And life is so advanced is where I'm from.
We've conquered fear and found Einstein was right,
Newton was wrong; space-time is relative,
And across the years a man can take flight
And find himself a new era to live.
The problem is career options are few;
In my time I'm a simple historian.
That's why I've come to 1592
In my sweet ride, a tricked-out DeLorean,
To write great plays and poetry sublime,
And prove to be the greatest of all time

Proof at last! Sadly, Shakespeare thought better of confessing the truth of his identity and turned this into the less revealing but far more beautiful (yawn) Sonnet 73.

The Epic Poems

What do we love about Shakespeare's four epic poems? Not much!

- They're not epic in the sense of terrific, they're epic in the sense of *long*, except that . . .
- Two of them, "A Lover's Complaint" and "The Phoenix and the Turtle," are both short. They're not remotely epic. Nor, unfortunately, are they remotely any good.
- The other two, "Venus and Adonis" and "The Rape of Lucrece," are still long, just not *Iliad* or *Odyssey* long. They're more technically called epyllions, but who wants to read a section titled "The Epyllions . . . Plus Two Other Poems That Are Longer Than Sonnets So We Couldn't Put Them There"?
- Whatever the four poems are collectively known as, nobody studies or reads them much anymore, which is too bad, because . . .
- They were meant to be read, not performed. It's much harder to read something than it is to have somebody else perform it for you.
- In his plays, Shakespeare had to contend with audiences who might not appreciate a scene or (even worse) actors who had trouble getting his words out of their mouths, forcing him to make changes he might not want to make. No such trouble with his poetry. He crafted his poems exactingly and probably supervised their publication, and thus he was able to make sure they appeared exactly as he meant them to be. He must have been doing something right: "Venus and Adonis" and "The Rape of Lucrece" were two of his most popular works during his lifetime.

Here's everything you need to know about Shakespeare's four nondramatic-and-not-exclusively-epic poems.

"Venus and Adonis"

This was the *Love Story* or *The Bridges of Madison County* of the late sixteenth century. It was hugely popular: Shakespeare was probably better known as the author of "Venus and Adonis" than he was as a playwright. The poem's also quite bawdy. It's worth a read just to see what got Elizabethan juices flowing. Here's a taste:

> *Backward she push'd him, as she would be thrust,*
> *And govern'd him in strength, though not in lust.*

Wow.

"The Rape of Lucrece"

Also hugely popular but in a different way, this poem has more in common with Shakespeare's later Tragedies. The imagery is brutal, the action savage: It shows Shakespeare developing a taste for the ol' ultraviolence. No wonder people loved it.

"A Lover's Complaint"

A minor work, which some scholars don't believe was written by Shakespeare. (Most do, however.) Move along, folks, nothing to see here.

"The Phoenix and the Turtle"

This is an allegorical work describing the death of two birds (the turtle is actually a turtledove) who may or may not represent Queen Elizabeth and her alleged sometime-lover, the Earl of Essex. It's just as good as all those children's theater shows your parents used to take you to. And no, that's not meant as a compliment.

POP QUIZ, HOTSHOT: *Which famous sexual come-on originated in "Venus and Adonis"?*

    A. "Let's get it on."
    B. "I'll smother thee with kisses."
    C. "I'm your Venus, I'm your fire / What's your desire?"
    D. "Shake it like a Polaroid picture."

Answer: B.

WHO WROTE THIS STUFF?

"For every expert, there is an equal and opposite expert."
—Arthur C. Clarke

Let's play another round of Unconventional Wisdom, shall we?

The Conventional Wisdom: There's very little evidence that William Shakespeare wrote the plays attributed to him.

The Reduced Wisdom: There's almost *no* evidence that Shakespeare wrote the plays attributed to him.

Oh sure, most people take it for granted that they were written by the "Bard of Stratford-upon-Avon," because that's what we've been told for hundreds of years. Shakespeare's name is printed on the title page of the First Folio. Why would everybody say it if it wasn't true?

Trouble is, there are more jokes about the authorship of Shakespeare's plays than there is solid evidence that he wrote them.

One dismissive quip admits that the plays weren't written by Shakespeare but by another writer of the same name. Many people claim they wrote Shakespeare even though Shakespeare never wrote back. And on the British television quiz show *Stake Your Claim*, Mr. Norman Voles of Gravesend stated emphatically, "I wrote all his plays, and my wife and I wrote his sonnets," a claim which fell to the ground when it was revealed that Mr. Voles was only forty-three (and when it was discovered on subsequent viewing that this was actually an old Monty Python sketch).

Fig. 17. The Reduced Shakespeare Company has determined scientifically that this is the most accurate portrait of William Shakespeare extant.

Nature abhors a vacuum. In the absence of definitive irrefutable proof that William Shakespeare actually wrote the plays that bear his name, entire cottage industries have grown up, setting out to prove that somebody else wrote them. The leading candidates are:

* Sir Francis Bacon
* Edward de Vere, Earl of Oxford
* William Stanley, Earl of Derby
* Roger Manners, Earl of Rutland
* Christopher Marlowe

There are many others. While some people graciously concede that Shakespeare *might* have written his own plays, the above-named candidates are those who have the largest international financing and the greatest array of scholars and nutjobs behind them.

And these are not late-twentieth-century-we're-obsessed-with-*The-X-Files*-conspiracy theories, either. These rumors and investigations have been going on for centuries. One of the earliest works to question Shakespeare's authorship was published in the early 1800s, long before the FBI covered up aliens in Roswell.

Critics of "authorship theorists" complain these "anti-Stratfordians" are iconoclasts and mischief-makers, ignoring the fact that iconoclasm and mischief-making are in the highest Shakespearean spirit. Shakespeare's plays are rich in deception and disguise; Shakespeare himself (whoever he was) even seems to toy with the authorship mystery in both *Hamlet* ("There are more things in heaven and earth, Horatio / Than are dreamt of in your philosophy") and *Romeo and Juliet* ("What's in a name? That which we call a rose by any other word would smell as sweet"). There's more going on here than any of you know, Shakespeare (or Bacon or Marlowe or whoever) seems to be hinting, and the author's name doesn't matter as long as the plays still smell. Which some of them do.

Let's briefly consider the leading candidates and examine their lives, their motives for hiding their identities, and the odds that one of these men indeed wrote the plays and sonnets of William Shakespeare.

Possible Authors of Shakespeare's Plays
A handy cheat sheet, in case you're too busy to read the rest of the chapter

Sir Francis Bacon
John Dryden
John Fletcher
Milli Vanilli
L. Ron Hubbard
Stephen King
Christopher Marlowe
Alan Smithee
The Hollywood Ten
Thomas Kyd
Edward De Vere, Earl of Oxford
William Stanley, Earl of Derby
Roger Manners, Earl of Rutland
Doris Kearns Goodwin
James Frey

Sir Francis Bacon (1561–1626)

Francis Bacon was a lawyer, statesman, historian, natural scientist, and philosopher. One of the arguments against Shakespeare as author is that, as a simple country landowner who lacked formal (and verifiable) education, there's no way he could so accurately portray the many philosophies and occupations that appear in the plays. Bacon, on the other hand, who declared "all knowledge" to be his province, is the one candidate who had the wide range of specialized knowledge that could have informed Shakespeare's writings.

Bacon was also gay, which, aside from being a virtual guarantee that he'd work in the theater, was also presumably something he'd wish to hide. Bacon's homosexuality would satisfy those who insist that Shakespeare's sonnets reveal the author's love for a man. And a life in the Elizabethan theater, filled with petty thieves and prostitutes, being, basically, almost the same disreputable business it is today, is something a man of Bacon's stature would definitely want to conceal.

Finally, and most convincingly of all, the word "bacon" means literally "little ham," which is merely another way of saying . . . wait for it . . . Hamlet. We rest our case.

ODDS (that Bacon wrote Shakespeare): 50–1.

Edward de Vere, Earl of Oxford (1550–1604)

The first man to argue that the seventeenth Earl of Oxford wrote the works of William Shakespeare was the unfortunately named J. Thomas Looney.

Looney believed that fiction is autobiography. And because what little is known of Shakespeare's life doesn't seem to have informed the plays or sonnets in the slightest, Looney found a guy whose life did. Like Hamlet, Edward de Vere was a highborn man at court who lost his father and felt dispossessed by the man who married his mother. Like Bertram in *All's Well That Ends Well* (and like many of the fallen aristocrats in Shakespeare's plays), de Vere was a wayward nobleman caught in an unhappy marriage, who traveled abroad and returned home. Like Bottom in *Midsummer*, de Vere had the head of a donkey, and like Caliban in *The Tempest*, de Vere was discovered, at his autopsy, to also be a mooncalf. The autobiographical parallels are eerie.

Even more convincing is the discovery of de Vere's copy of the Bible, which now belongs to the Folger Shakespeare Library in Washington, D.C. It's actually filled with hundreds of markings, highlighted words, and underlined passages in de Vere's own hand, many of which can also be found in Shakespeare's works.

This would appear to be what we historians call evidence: one of Shakespeare's actual resources. One can imagine this copy of the Bible sitting on Shakespeare's writing table, occasionally being flipped through as the great author searched for the perfect phrase or devastating *bon mot*. It's particularly exciting to those frustrated by the fact that William Shakespeare of Stratford left behind no writings in his own hand: no first drafts, no notes or scrawled-out passages, no heavily marked copies of the books he was stealing all his best stuff from; not even any letters to his loved ones or his family—nothing, in fact, not one single solitary scrap of paper to indicate he was a writer at all or, indeed, could even read. Edward de Vere, the Earl of Oxford, at least leaves a *tiny* paper trail.

And most convincing of all is de Vere's coat of arms, which depicts a lion shaking a broken spear. Get it? A shakespear! We call that a smoking gun, my friends![51]

ODDS: 20–1.

William Stanley, Earl of Derby (1561–1642)

The authorship question is one of history's great controversies, so naturally it involves the French.

Professor Abel Lefranc of the College de France was a respected authority on Rabelais, Moliere, and the literature of the seventeenth and eighteenth centuries. Like the giggle-inducing Tom Looney, Lefranc concluded that, unlike every single writer ever known to have existed, there is no relationship between Shakespeare's life and his works. But unlike Looney, Lefranc was a well-respected literary scholar and wasn't laughed right out of the patisserie.[52]

Lefranc found a man whose life did seem to inform at least two of Shakespeare's plays: William Stanley, the sixth Earl of Derby.[53] Stanley was an aristocrat who studied law and is known to have spent about five years in Europe in the 1580s, where he killed a man in a duel in Spain, and traveled extensively in France.

But what really seals the deal is that an Englishman is known to have visited the court of Navarre in France, observing and participating in events that mirror exactly the action in *Love's Labour's Lost* (see synopsis, page 82). For Lefranc (and others who think like him), that Englishman was almost undoubtedly William Stanley.

---

[51] Sorry, did we say "most convincing"? We meant "most silly."

[52] We won't even mention the French radicals who tie up traffic all over Europe, claiming that "Shakespeare" is simply an Anglicization of the true author's French name: "Jacques Pierre."

[53] "Who the hell is that?!" you cry, and you're absolutely right. History is filled with people you've never heard of, and every single one of them lived a life more recorded and better documented than the "famous" William Shakespeare. It's maddening.

According to John Michell, the author of *Who Wrote Shakespeare?* ("Best overview yet of the authorship controversy" — *Washington Post*) the only difference between the play and what really happened is that Shakespeare (or Stanley) changed the king of Navarre's name from Henri to Ferdinand (the name of Stanley's older brother, as it happens) and the visitor to the court became the daughter of the king in the play rather than his real-life estranged wife; a princess, in other words, instead of a queen.

The play also contains the character of Holofernes, a ridiculously pedantic schoolmaster, who is a spot-on caricature of Stanley's tutor and chaperone. This, as well as dozens of other specific details, make many scholars feel that the events from *Love's Labour's Lost* were observed from life by William Stanley rather than "merely" imagined by somebody else.

The Tempest also matches details of Stanley's life. The "brave new world" that Miranda mentions has often been taken to mean America, indicating that Sir Walter Raleigh was the inspiration for Prospero (and possibly the author of Shakespeare's plays, but let's not even go there). But the "rocky crag" of Prospero's island more closely resembles the Calf of Man, located just off the coast of the Isle of Man, in the Irish Sea between England and Ireland. The Calf of Man is a mile wide, filled with caves, inlets, and fresh water, and has caused many shipwrecks over the years. It's exactly the way Prospero's island is described in *The Tempest*.

"So what?" you ask. So this: William Stanley was the hereditary king of the Isle of Man, ruling it jointly with the Countess of Derby by governmental decree. Who else would know or could describe the uninhabited Calf of Man better?

And, as has already been mentioned, Stanley's older brother Ferdinando has the exact same name[54] of the prince who marries Prospero's daughter.

And the dedication of the First Folio is signed with the initials W. S., which obviously stand for William Stanley! What other name could those initials possibly stand for?[55]

---

[54] Almost.
[55] William Shakespeare.

Is all this evidence incredibly circumstantial . . . that is, persuasive . . . or what? [56]

ODDS: 10–1.

Roger Manners, Earl of Rutland (1576–1612)

"Why do all the candidates have to be earls?" is the logical question, and we're tired of hearing it. The answer is: Because the most critical Shakespearean scholars (sorry, we mean iconoclastic anti-Stratfordians) insist that in order to write about so many aristocrats and educated people, Shakespeare must have been one himself.

Textual clues tell us that the author of Shakespeare's plays had a classical education, probably from Cambridge. Hey, you know what? Roger Manners, Earl of Rutland, went to Cambridge! (As did Bacon and Oxford.) A common theme in Shakespeare's plays is two brothers who hate each other. Hey, you know what? Roger Manners, Earl of Rutland, hated his brothers and confiscated the lands of one of them, just as Oliver did to Orlando in *As You Like It*! Every Shakespeare scholar (even the orthodox Stratfordians) believes that the author must have traveled throughout Europe and spent extensive time in Italy. Hey, you know what? Roger Manners, Earl of Rutland, studied at Padua University, in addition to Cambridge!

But we've saved the best for last. The author of *Hamlet* must have gone to Denmark: It's described too accurately for someone to have simply "made up" the details. Well, you know what? Roger Manners, Earl of Rutland, went to Denmark! He headed up an English delegation to Denmark under James I, visited Elsinore Castle, and—*and!*—had two classmates at Padua University named . . . drum roll, please . . . *Rosencrantz and Guildenstern!*[57]

---

[56] What.

[57] Absolutely true, according to John Michell in *Who Wrote Shakespeare?* Complete and utter bollocks (our words, not his), according to Bertram Fields in *Players*. Shoot. Every party has a pooper.

The problem with Rutland, however, and it's a big one, is that "Venus and Adonis," as well as four of Shakespeare's plays, were written before Rutland was twenty years old.

In other words, Rutland would have had to be a genius, a child prodigy.

Well, that's ridiculous. We can accept William Shakespeare as an uneducated landowner whose genius sprang forth extempore from his mother wit. But Roger Manners? That's just crazy talk.

ODDS: 70–1.

Christopher Marlowe (1564–93)

The biggest question advocates have to answer in putting forth their respective candidates for authorship is, "Why?" *Why* did Bacon/Oxford/Derby/Rutland have to hide their great genius? *Why* were they forced to create an elaborate conspiracy to have their plays produced and published under a false identity? Why wouldn't they all stand up proudly and proclaim "I am Spartacus . . . I mean, Shakespeare!"?

The answer's always pretty much, well, the theater's a disreputable business, I'm far too well-bred to be seen associating with that crowd, I don't want to embarrass my family, I'm gay, I'm a nobleman, I'm a gay nobleman—you know, stuff like that.

Christopher Marlowe is the only candidate with an answer (and it's a great one) as to why he would hide his genius and participate in an elaborate conspiracy.

Why? Because Marlowe was *dead*.

Marlowe was killed in a Deptford tavern brawl in 1593. Or was he? John Michell, the author of *Who Wrote Shakespeare?*, calls Marlowe "the professional candidate" because Marlowe's the only possible author of Shakespeare's plays who really was a playwright himself and not "a noble dilettante." But Michell misses the double meaning of the word "professional" (or does he?) because Marlowe was something else.

Marlowe was also a professional spy.

At some point while he was at Cambridge (hey, look who else went to Cambridge!), Marlowe became a member of (cue the

James Bond music) Her Majesty's Secret Service. Before he grad-
uated, Marlowe left school and entered a Jesuit seminary in
Rheims, which was a hotbed of Catholic intrigue against Queen
Elizabeth, a Protestant. His secret mission was apparently to report on potential plots against the queen, but it was assumed that
Marlowe himself was engaged in treasonous activities; consequently, Cambridge withheld Marlowe's degree.

But the Cambridge authorities received an extraordinary letter from the Privy Council, the queen's cabinet. The council's
letter said that,

> . . . in all his actions [Marlowe] had behaved him selfe orderlie and
> discreetlie wherebie he had done her Majestie good service and de-
> served to be rewarded for his faithful dealinge . . .

And that

> . . . it was not her Majesties pleasure that anie one emploied as he
> had been in matters touching the benefitt of his Countrie should be
> defamed by those that are ignorant in th' affaires he went about.

The details are vague, but one thing is certain: Only sinister con-
spiratorial men would spell that badly.

But Marlowe got his degree. He also continued to make
enemies on pretty much every level of English society. He
hung with a fast, free-thinking crowd that included Sir Walter Raleigh and debated many of the issues of the day, including those which, like religion, were forbidden. Marlowe's
pronouncements as part of his clique brought him a summons
to appear immediately before the Court of Star Chamber in
London, under the charge of "atheism." This was not good
news: Charges of "atheism" and "blasphemy" had a way of becoming punishable by death under the more general heading
of "treason," and the Star Chamber was not above torturing
its defendants to get whatever information they needed.[58]

But Marlowe had at least one powerful friend: Thomas Walsingham, who was the cousin of the creator of the queen's secret

---

[58] That's how they got Marlowe's name: They tortured his friend and fellow
playwright Thomas Kyd to obtain it.

service, Sir Francis Walsingham, and something of a master spy himself. Walsingham's been described as Marlowe's "patron" and sometimes his "employer"; they were definitely "roommates" so it's probably not too far off to call them "boyfriends." In any event, they must have been very close because, somehow, Marlowe was released on bail and not, as Thomas Kyd had been, sent to prison and stretched on the rack. His trial was set to begin on June 1.

On May 30, the day before his trial, Marlowe was killed in a tavern brawl, apparently in a dispute over who was going to pay the check. Yeah, sure: Marlowe attacked somebody over a few pence the day before he was going on trial for his life.

There are other problems:

- The "tavern," as described in the coroner's report, was actually a respectable house owned by Dame Eleanor Bull, whose sister was the goddaughter of Queen Elizabeth's nanny![59]
- The four men involved in this "brawl" were all employed by or associated with master spy Thomas Walsingham!
- Ingram Frizer, the one who stabbed Marlowe, immediately resumed working for Walsingham, even though he had just killed Walsingham's "dear friend" and "admired poet"!
- There's no way Oswald could have got off that many rounds from a single-action rifle. Not even highly trained army sharpshooters can do that![60]

In any event, the story of Marlowe's death, like a paper rowboat, doesn't hold water. Neither the facts of the case nor the logic of the official explanation make any sense.

And then there's the textual evidence. Many scholars, including boring, non-conspiracy-loving ones, acknowledge the influence Marlowe "must have" had on the young William Shakespeare.[61] Others note the possibility that Marlowe wrote

---

[59] If that doesn't reek of privilege and evil, what does?

[60] Sorry. Wrong conspiracy.

[61] For example: "Marlowe's *Dr. Faustus* was the first work that bore the unmistakable impress of that tragic power that was to find its highest embodiment in *King Lear, Macbeth, Hamlet,* and *Othello.*" — Charles Grant, quoted in *The Murder of the Man Who Was Shakespeare.*

some or all of Shakespeare's *Titus Andronicus, Richard II, Richard III,* and the three parts of *Henry VI.* Still others further claim that Marlowe wrote *The Comedy of Errors,* much of *Henry V,* the balcony scene of *Romeo and Juliet,* and every fourth word of *Troilus and Cressida.* These people are referred to as "nuts."

However, there's a sound technical basis for the claim that Marlowe wrote Shakespeare's plays, as well as statistical evidence to back it up. In the nineteenth century, Dr. Thomas Mendenhall, a noted physicist who served as president of the American Association for the Advancement of Science, devised a method whereby an author's individual writing style could be charted and drawn on a graph. Mendenhall's goal was to determine an author's unconscious, inherent, and unchanging predisposition toward using anywhere from one to fifteen-letter words. Mendenhall counted every letter of every word written by Shelley, Keats, Sir Walter Scott, William Thackeray, and Lord Byron—by hand. (This was BC, remember: Before Computers.) The tests were compared and analyzed. The result? No two authors are alike. The conclusion? No two authors will, mechanically, unconsciously, write identically.

Word of Mendenhall's conclusions spread, and he was asked to apply his method in order to prove that Francis Bacon wrote Shakespeare's plays. In order to create a large enough sample, Mendenhall counted (again, BC) every letter of every word written by Bacon, Shakespeare, Ben Jonson, Goldsmith, Beaumont, Fletcher, Marlowe, Lytton, and Addison.[62]

Mendenhall discovered that Shakespeare's vocabulary consisted of words averaging four letters in length.[63] But Shakespeare's four-letter-word average was something Mendenhall had never seen before in any other writer. Bacon, for example, used much longer words, and every other writer had his own average word length and unique stylistic oddities. The Baconian who hired Mendenhall was very disappointed. But then as Mendenhall reported:

---

[62] Who? Lytton? Addison? Doesn't matter.
[63] Big deal. Playwright David Mamet uses a lot of four-letter words, too.

It was in the counting and plotting of the plays of Christopher Marlowe, however, that something akin to a sensation was produced . . . In the characteristic curve of his plays *Christopher Marlowe agrees with Shakespeare as well as Shakespeare agrees with himself.*[64]

In the words of Shakespearean scholar Scooby-Doo, "Rhuh?!?"

According to Mendenhall, Marlowe and Shakespeare have the exact same literary fingerprint, something no two other authors, subjected to the same scientific scrutiny, have ever demonstrated.

And here's another fun fact: Marlowe "died" on May 30, 1593. The name "William Shakespeare" made its very first appearance in connection with a dramatic work only four months later in September 1593, when "Venus and Adonis" was registered (as all books were required to be) at the Stationer's Office, sort of an Elizabethan copyright office. And many of the scholars who conclude Shakespeare must have spent time in Italy believe he probably went there in . . . ta-da! . . .1593.

So here's what probably happened: Marlowe was a spy for Queen Elizabeth's government; his work was so valuable to Her Majesty that the Privy Council interceded in order for him to get his degree; his free-thinking intellectual ways ultimately made him a liability; his friend/lover Thomas Walsingham arranged both the "murder" of Marlowe and the speediest inquest and acquittal in the history of Elizabethan jurisprudence so that Marlowe could escape to Italy and continue to write the plays and sonnets that fueled his soul; which he then gradually had produced and published under the name of the sometime actor and Stratford landowner, William Shakespeare.

Whew.

It may not be the most convincing of the various theories presented here, but it's definitely the coolest.[65]

---

[64] Emphasis, obviously, added.

[65] We suppose it's possible that Marlowe was murdered by Walsingham's men simply because he was becoming an embarrassment and a political liability, but where's the fun in that? We're from the Oliver Stone school: We prefer a ridiculously far-fetched conspiracy every time.

ODDS: 100–1.

ODDS (if you accept that Marlowe faked his own death, which should be easy because you already accept one of two equally outlandish possibilities: a) that an uneducated Stratford landowner wrote the greatest dramatic literature in the history of language; or b) a vast Elizabethan cabal conspired to hide the identity of the man who *truly* wrote the greatest dramatic literature in the history of language): **Even money.**

And what of William Shakespeare? What about the possibility that Shakespeare wrote all those keen plays and nifty sonnets himself?

Good point.

William Shakespeare (1564–1616)

There is just the tiniest bit of evidence to support this craziest of all theories—that someone named William Shakespeare actually wrote the works of William Shakespeare—and that's a little thing we like to call *logic*.

First of all, while conspiracies are fun, they're difficult to keep quiet. Dozens, if not hundreds of Elizabethans would have been in on the charade, and so would their families and descendants. *Not one of them has ever mentioned anything.* (We asked.) If Shakespeare didn't write these plays, it's the best-kept secret in history.

Second, isn't there evidence that Shakespeare wrote Shakespeare? Well, his name's on the First Folio, the first collection of his plays that was published only seven years after his death. His picture appears there, too. That seems . . . evidential.

And third, apparently everyone he worked with professionally knew he wrote the plays. In fact, it was two longtime colleagues, John Hemminges and Henry Condell, who compiled and edited the First Folio. And famed playwright Ben Jonson, a friend and colleague of the Bard, wrote a glowing tribute to Shakespeare as an introduction to the book.

Then there's the little matter of the monument in Stratford. Evidently, the people in Shakespeare's hometown believed he wrote the plays. Shortly after his death, they built an elaborate marble and limestone monument to Shakespeare in the Church of the Holy Trinity.

In *In Search of Shakespeare*, Michael Wood points out that the plays contain (to use some highly technical academic jargon) lots and lots of Warwickshire phrases and spelling.

And (where are we?) *sixth*, if you play the Beatles' "Revolution #9" from the White Album backward (which is much more difficult with a CD than it was with an LP), you can distinctly hear the words, "Shakespeare wrote Shakespeare. Shakespeare wrote Shakespeare."

But despite all this blazingly clear evidence, some people simply won't accept the obvious. They've been searching and digging for hundreds of years, desperate to prove that someone else wrote Shakespeare's plays, and they have yet to find a smoking gun. These folks are evidently smoking something else entirely.

ODDS: Even money.

So who wrote Shakespeare's plays?

Well, this whole book is testament to the fact that Shakespeare's won the day. Entire industries—British tourism, publishing houses, and Shakespeare companies from the Royal to the Reduced—all depend on the strength and survival of that precious illusion. As William Shakespeare himself put it so magnificently in his screenplay for *The Man Who Shot Liberty Valance*, "When the legend becomes fact, print the legend."

Yes, there are lots of facts, much evidence (not all of it, unfortunately, in Shakespeare's favor), many theories, and endless suppositions as to who wrote the works of Shakespeare. Anyone arrogant enough to claim that only one verdict is possible from all the available evidence is a fool.

For surely, there's only one verdict possible from all the available evidence: William Shakespeare was a time traveler from the future, a strange visitor from another century with powers and abilities far beyond those of mortal men. William Shakespeare—armed with poetic and dramatic works so ingenious and transporting they changed the world. William Shakespeare—who left his rough drafts and discarded scenes at his home in the distant future; and who, when he departed the early seventeenth century, took his original manuscripts back to his own time, a time so far ahead we haven't reached it yet, thus explaining why we have yet to discover a single manuscript or page bearing his signature or any of his brilliant writings in his own genius hand.

You wait. It's the only possible solution.

SHAKESPEARE'S CONTEMPORARIES

Some people even argue that Shakespeare's fellow professional playwrights Thomas Kyd, John Webster, and Ben Jonson might have written Shakespeare's plays, but only fools believe that. Like us.

Thomas Kyd 1558–94
- Nickname: "Sporting Kyd"
- Best known plays: *The Spanish Tragedy*
- In free time: named names under torture, giving up former roommate Kit Marlowe
- Wrote all of Shakespeare's plays

Christopher Marlowe 1564–93
- Nickname: Kit
- Best known plays: *Tamburlaine the Great, The Jew of Malta*
- In free time: was spy for Her Majesty's Secret Service
- Wrote all of Shakespeare's plays

John Webster 1580–1630
- Nickname: Webby
- Best known plays: *The Duchess of Malfi, The White Devil*
- In free time: Unsuccessful ambulance-chasing lawyer; unsuccessful because ambulances hadn't been invented yet
- Wrote all of Shakespeare's plays

Ben Jonson 1572–1637
- Nickname: LL Ben J
- Best known plays: *Volpone, The Alchemist, Every Man In His Humour*
- In free time: won Best Supporting Actor Academy Award for *The Last Picture Show* and the Gold Medal in the 1988 Olympics 100-meter dash (he was disqualified for steroids)
- Wrote all of Shakespeare's plays

SHAKESPEARE, INC.

"Oh, had I but followed the arts!"
Twelfth Night, Act I, Scene 3

hakespeare followed the arts, and look where it got him.

A steady gig with an acting company. A share of the profits. Patronage from some of the most powerful men in England. Cuddling and licky-face from some of the most powerful men in England, as well as at least one Dark Lady. A coat of arms and the status of a gentleman. The biggest house in Stratford. And that was just while he was alive. After he died, he achieved worldwide fame as the greatest English-language writer who ever lived.

But let's back up. Let's accept, for the sake of argument, that Shakespeare did indeed write the plays for which he is credited. As we've mentioned, how a man of his background managed to write so many great plays is a mystery.

But if Shakespeare was a genius to write the plays, what kind of supercolossal, *über*-genius must he have been to parlay some pretty decent drama into the multibillion-dollar Shakespeare industry he has become today? It's an incomparable achievement, especially if you consider that he didn't really start marketing himself beyond his writings until several years after he died.

Shakespeare has become a big industry: Shakespeare festivals, Shakespeare theaters, Shakespeare movies, Shakespeare tours, Shakespeare historic sites, Shakespeare companies, Shakespeare books, and Shakespeare action figures. How did this happen?

Shakespeare followed the example of other performers who had success in posthumous self-marketing. James Dean and Marilyn

Fig. 18. William Shakespeare today.

Monroe were especially inspirational to Shakespeare. They managed to create a body of work and then die young in tragic circumstances. Shakespeare arranged to die at age fifty-two—not young, but not old, either. He apparently drank himself silly with his buddies, Ben Jonson and John Drayton, which led to a fever and death. Shakespeare's death was not as tragic as dying in a car crash or being poisoned by the CIA but, for Elizabethan times, it wasn't bad. And as in the death of Marilyn, the Kennedys' involvement in Shakespeare's death has been implicated but never proven.

Okay, so now you're a quasi-celebrity and have managed to die fairly young. What's your next move? It's easy. Destroy the evidence. Shakespeare left no paper trail: No books, no papers, no early drafts of his work. Why? He wanted to create doubt and mystique. Did he ever really exist? Did he write the plays? Was his true love Joe DiMaggio or Arthur Miller? We'll never know.

Next, he followed James Dean's example and released some of his work posthumously. In Dean's case, it was the movie *Giant*. In Shakespeare's, it was the First Folio of 1623, published seven years after his death.

Then, slowly but surely, he began to leave little clues here and there that maybe he didn't write the plays. He hired wackos to write entire books theorizing about who was the *real* author of Shakespeare's work. This evolved into an entire Shakespeare-conspiracy cottage industry.

Then, like Elvis, Shakespeare opened up his home for tours. Inspired by the way Elvis put Memphis on the celebrity map, Shakespeare's did the same thing with Stratford-upon-Avon.

But Shakespeare did the King one better. He opened up not only his own house for tours, but his mother's, Mary Arden's, house, as well. And in conjunction with the British royal family, he started a theater company in Stratford named after himself, the Royal Shakespeare Company. At this point, the money really began to pour in. Shakespeare became a brand name. Everybody wanted a piece of him.[66]

FUN FACT: For more than two centuries, the house that had been listed on the Stratford tourist map as Mary Arden's house was the wrong one. A few years ago, it was discovered that she lived in the house next door, on Glebe Farm.

Fig. 19. Mary Arden's House in Stratford. Ground Zero in the Shakespeare Tourism Industry.

Now here we are, four hundred years later, and the Shakespeare business is in better shape than ever. Let's take a look at the state of Shakespeare, Inc. today, shall we?

Shakespeare Festivals

Today, virtually every town in the English-speaking world has its own Shakespeare festival. How did the Bard of Avon become the McDonald's of culture, you ask? The answer is simple: young people in love. Shakespeare festivals exist for young couples to sit under the stars, drink wine, cuddle under a blanket, and get a little culture.[67] Oh, sure, there are a handful of real Shakespeare fans, but they don't go to see the local amateurs. They go to the big city. The small local companies abound because of their romantic atmosphere and free-flowing booze.

Shakespeare Companies

There are many excellent Shakespeare companies out there, as well as many unscrupulous companies that've only attached

---

[66] Hmm. Shakespeare relics. That's an idea worth exploring.

[67] Yes, in the vernacular of today's youth it's called "getting a little culture." If one is indiscriminate about where they get their "culture," they may have to get a culture to see what they got.

Shakespeare to their name for the sake of credibility. Buyer beware! Check out the helpful list below:

Ten Excellent Shakespeare Companies

Royal Shakespeare Company—Stratford-upon-Avon, England
Royal National Theater of Britain—London, England
Stratford Festival—Stratford-not-upon-Avon-
    but-in-Ontario, Canada
Oregon Shakespeare Festival—Ashland, Oregon
New York Shakespeare Festival—New York, New York
Old Globe Theater—San Diego, California
Folger Shakespeare Theater—Washington, D.C.
Shakespeare's Globe—London
Troubador Theater Company—Los Angeles, California[68]
Reduced Shakespeare Company—The World

Eight Shakespeare Companies to Avoid

National Shakespeare Theater for the Incontinent
Leroy's Shakespeare 'n' Barbecue
Shakespeare 'R' Us
Anything by Robert Wilson, Shakespearean or not
Smorgas Bard—All You Can Watch
Frank's One-Man Shakespeare Festival in the Restroom
The McShakespeare Drive-Thru
Billy Bob's Monster Truck and Shakespeare Rally

Shakespeare Historic Sites and Tours

Shakespeare tourism is at an all-time high. London has been largely reconstructed to look exactly like it did in Shakespeare's

---

[68] The "Troubies" combine the wonder of Shakespeare's poetry with the majesty of 1970s and 1980s pop. Their masterpieces include *Twelfth Dog Night, A Midsummer Saturday Night's Fever Dream, Romeo Hall and Juliet Oates, Fleetwood Macbeth, The Comedy of Aerosmith,* and *Hamlet—The Artist Formerly Known as Prince of Denmark.*

☼ Tips for Enjoying an Evening of ✪outdoor Shakespeare

1. Bring lots of coffee.
2. Bring a cushion to sit on.
3. Bring a blanket.
4. Bring a babe.
5. Read a synopsis of the play ahead of time so you'll know what the heck is going on.
6. Make sure it's a first-rate company doing a good production (read the reviews!) of an accessible play (see page 113).
7. Use the toilet before the play begins.*
8. Take a nap that afternoon before the show.
9. Take a nap that evening during Act III.

*See tip #1

time, as has Stratford-upon-Avon.

In London, there's the reconstructed Globe Theater on the Southbank of the Thames, as well as the Royal Shakespeare Company. The National Theater also performs a great deal of Shakespeare, as does the Open Air Theater in Regents Park.

In Stratford, you can visit Shakespeare's home, his mother's home, and the Royal Shakespeare Company's Stratford theaters. But by far the best, tackiest, and least authentic Shakespearean site is the animatronic tourist trap that takes you back to Shakespeare's time. You stand in this room and through the nonmiracles of bad lighting, scratchy recordings and phony-looking mannequins, you discover what Elizabethan life was really like. We cannot recommend it highly enough.

And Shakespeare tourism is not limited to England. Reconstructed versions of Elizabethan theaters (of widely varying degrees of accuracy and quality) are spread across the globe, from Hollywood to Tokyo to Ashland, Oregon.

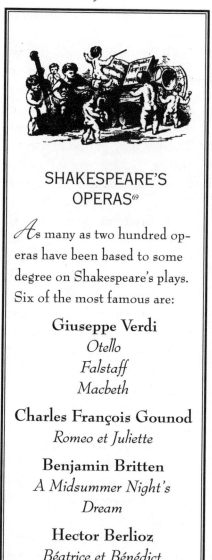

SHAKESPEARE'S OPERAS[69]

*A*s many as two hundred operas have been based to some degree on Shakespeare's plays. Six of the most famous are:

Giuseppe Verdi
Otello
Falstaff
Macbeth

Charles François Gounod
Romeo et Juliette

Benjamin Britten
A Midsummer Night's Dream

Hector Berlioz
Béatrice et Bénédict

And in Montgomery, Alabama, on the grounds of the Alabama Shakespeare Festival, a Shakespeare garden grows all the plants and flowers that Shakespeare mentions in his plays.

Shakespeare Books

A quick search at Amazon.com will show you an overwhelming number of books about Shakespeare. Lots of them are of questionable quality and scholarship.[70] But for a list of books that we recommend, check out the bibliography at the end of this book. A word of warning: Lots of Shakespeare books are just an excuse to throw a bunch of stuff together to make a quick buck.[71] Reader, beware!

Shakespeare Merchandise

We've seen Shakespeare action figures. Really. And Shakespeare finger puppets.

---

[69] Warning: Opera can be dangerous to your health and may cause drowsiness. Do not drive or operate heavy machinery while watching opera. Before purchasing opera tickets, please consult your physician.

[70] Like the book you are currently reading.

[71] Like the book you are currently reading.

And Shakespeare rubber ducks. And animated Shakespeare cartoons. And Shakespeare T-shirts and posters and baseball hats and tea towels. We even know a guy from Los Angeles who makes a living as a Shakespeare impersonator. Okay, he's not a piece of merchandise, but he is a piece of work.

The best places to find Shakespeare toys, gifts, and doodads are in the gift shops of major Shakespeare theaters. In Stratford-upon-Avon there are Shakespeare gift shops on every block. But there's always room for more merchandise. Here are a few suggestions:

The *King John* PortaPotti

A *Midsummer Night's Dream* sleeping pills

Julius Caesar salad dressing

Hamlet: the world's smallest ham

The *Comedy of Errors* guide to Washington politics

Taming of the Shrew miniseries: *The Martha Stewart Story*

Measure for Measure yardsticks

The *Henry VIII* do-it-yourself divorce kit (chopping block not included)

Shakespeare's Movies

And then there are Shakespeare's movies, probably the largest and most lucrative division of Shakespeare, Inc. In fact, the Shakespeare movie business is so big, it gets its own chapter.

Are you ready? Lights, camera, Shakespeare!

THE FILMS OF
WILLIAM SHAKESPEARE

"If Shakespeare were alive today,
he'd have a three-picture deal at Warner Brothers."
—Marc Norman, co-author, *Shakespeare in Love*

hen Shakespeare decided
to be born in 1564, he
only really considered
one other era: today.

With film the dominant entertainment medium of the twentieth century and DVDs the most profitable of the twenty-first, you know Shakespeare would be right in the thick of it, with his ear to the ground and his finger on the pulse of the global public. Forget about entertaining thousands of people in his small wooden O; with the rise of electronic technology, he could be entertaining *billions* around the world with a variety of film and television projects.

And the funny thing is, he *is*.[72]

At the end of the nineteenth century, fledgling movie producers tried to film Shakespeare's works in the hope it might legitimize their upstart medium by hitching it to his established cultural coattails. Thus, we have bizarre-looking recordings of famous nineteenth-century actors declaiming Shakespeare's most famous speeches—silently. They're fascinating as historical documents but not very entertaining.

---

[72] And his love of language would be sated by his dominance as hip-hop mogul and recording artist, Shakezpeare.

Things changed slightly with the advent of sound. Movies were called "talkies" then, and if there's one thing we know about Shakespeare, it's that the brother could *talk*. Less innovative producers, however, forgot that movies are also supposed to *move*, which made for a lot of stagy, not very compelling films.

But there are great movie versions of Shakespeare's plays out there, which can be wonderful introductions for the novice, rewarding for the serious student, and just plain entertaining for the casual viewer with maybe not that much interest in Shakespeare at all. We list them (like the plays, alphabetically) on the following pages, comparing and contrasting different versions, and we try to focus on how they work as *movies*, not how they succeed (or don't) in translating Shakespeare to the big screen. Our list isn't complete by any means: We've tried to focus on the movies you might actually want to watch, and left the obscure black-and-white Finnish/Eskimo musical adaptations sung in Esperanto to a more thoughtful publication.

The BBC Shakespeare

In the late 1970s, the British Broadcasting Company (BBC) embarked on an ambitious scheme to videotape and broadcast all thirty-nine of Shakespeare's plays. It's a remarkable achievement, a complete permanent record using mostly complete texts, and providing in some cases the only recorded versions of several of Shakespeare's neglected, lesser plays.

They're also, it must be said, not great. Shot mostly indoors on studio sets, using excellent actors but budgets of about 23 pence, they're not what you expect when you sit down to watch a movie. Nonetheless, they might in many cases be your best option if it's impossible to find a good live production near you. They're also available in handsomely designed DVD boxed sets (divided into Comedies, Tragedies, and Histories; suitable for gifting or re-gifting), so, if nothing else, they'll look terrific on your bookshelf.

ALL'S WELL THAT ENDS WELL
Film Versions: Seven[73]
Notable Film Versions: None
The finest film adaptation is probably *Oil's Well That Ends Well*, starring the Three Stooges and featuring an unusually strong performance by Joe Besser as Helena.
Rating: 🩇 🩇 🩇 🩇 🩇

ANTONY AND CLEOPATRA
Film Versions: Six
Notable Film Versions: One
Directed by Trevor Nunn (1974)
Richard Johnson as Marc Antony
Janet Suzman as Cleopatra
Corin Redgrave as Octavius Caesar
Patrick Stewart as Enobarbus
A sequel of sorts to *Julius Caesar* (it's the same Marc Antony), this play should really be called *Antony and Octavius*, but Shakespeare the marketing genius knew that the Egyptian queen is who the audience really wants to see. It's true in this film version, as well: Janet Suzman is everything you want in a Cleopatra, and she totally dominates the proceedings. You miss her when the other scenes focus endlessly on the conflict between the Roman politicians (as embodied by Corin Redgrave's icy Octavius Caesar) and the soldiers in the field (embodied by Richard Johnson as Antony and Patrick Stewart acting beautifully behind the ugliest fake beard and wig in the history of show business).

The movie's good but can't disguise the fact that it's not a great play. It doesn't approach the passion of *Romeo and Juliet*, the historical introspection of *Henry V*, or the tragedy of *Hamlet*. You sense Shakespeare trying to use bits that worked before and—despite some great lines ("Age cannot wither her, nor

---

[73] Refers to the number of adaptations listed on the Internet Movie Database (IMDb).

custom stale her infinite variety," Act II, Scene 2)—mostly not succeeding.

Rating: 💀 💀

We should also mention that there's a hard-to-find 1983 TV film that features a cast of literally dozens, with actors as varied as Timothy Dalton and Lynn Redgrave (Corin's and Vanessa's sister), down to Anthony Geary (Luke from *General Hospital*) and *Star Trek's* Walter Koenig and Nichelle Nichols. It sounds positively camptastic.

AS YOU LIKE IT
Film Versions: Ten
Notable Film Versions: One
Directed by Kenneth Branagh (2006)
Brian Blessed as the Duke
Kevin Kline as Jaques
Bryce Dallas Howard as Rosalind
Rating: 💀 💀 💀 💀 💀

There's a modern-day adaptation by Christine Edzard that received mixed reviews and is impossible to find, and the BBC version stars always-wonderful Helen Mirren, but only Branagh's version does big-screen justice to one of Shakespeare's most likable comedies. Channeling his inner Kurosawa and setting it among British colonials in nineteenth-century Japan, Branagh fills the forest of Arden with cherry blossoms and creates a sumo wrestling match filled with *Crouching Tiger, Hidden Shakespeare*–type martial arts.

Bryce Dallas Howard (Ron's daughter) makes a lovely and contemporary-feeling Rosalind; her scenes with Adrian Lester (from *Primary Colors* and Branagh's *Love's Labour's Lost*) have a delightful joie de vivre, and you can believe Orlando doesn't know that "Ganymede" is really a girl. Almost. Alfred Molina (Doc Ock from *Spider-Man 2*) and Janet McTeer (from nothing you've ever seen) are wonderful as the older lovers. Brian Blessed brings his customary authority to the role of the Duke. And Kevin Kline is perfect in the role of Jaques—his "All the world's a stage" speech is finally captured on film in all its wise and world-weary wit. Wonderful. Branagh's done it again![74]

THE COMEDY OF ERRORS
Film Versions: Eight
Notable Film Versions: None

Almost all the movie versions of *Comedy* were filmed for TV—consequently, they're all pretty stagy. Very little effort was put into adapting the plays for a different medium. Let's put it this way: every expense was spared. This includes the BBC version that cast comic legend Roger Daltrey (yes, the lead singer of the Who: *that* comic legend) as *both* Dromios. Therefore, it *must* be brilliant, right?

ESSAY QUESTION: *Is the plural for Dromio, Dromii? Why not? Discuss.*

CORIOLANUS
Film Versions: Eight
Notable Film Versions: None

If you can find it, there's the Joseph Papp–produced New York Shakespeare Festival stage version out there, apparently on film, with Morgan Freeman as Coriolanus. Freeman can do no wrong, so it's definitely worth a look.

CYMBELINE
Film Versions: Four
Notable Film Versions: None

The version directed by Patrick Tucker listed on IMDb is incorrect. It was a stage production that featured co-author Reed Martin and many of our UC Berkeley classmates, but as far as we know, it was never filmed. Wait—unless it *was* filmed, and they didn't want to use Reed in the movie! (That would make sense, actually.) Oh, treachery! Seek it out!

---

[74] We haven't seen it, and the movie hasn't been released as this book's going to press. We're crossing our fingers and praying it's more like Branagh's *Much Ado* and less like his *Frankenstein*.

HAMLET

Film Versions: More than fifty
Notable Film Versions: How much time do you have?

As the famous catchphrase has it, *now* we're cooking with gas! There's a *Hamlet* out there for every taste: tragic, comedic, historical, pastoral, pastoral-comical, historical-pastoral . . . [75] We're sure there's one that's right for you.

Hamlet's a great play: Everybody says it. The reason we happen to agree is that we watched the following film versions, and in every one of them, even the less successful ones, the play holds up. There are no ridiculous plot points to accept,[76] no unbelievable disguises to buy: Just a hero struggling, a villain scheming, and a family tormented by personal and political intrigue. Pretty simple, really.

Hamlet (1948)
Directed by Laurence Olivier
Laurence Olivier as Hamlet, Prince of Denmark
Basil Sydney as Claudius, the king
Eileen Herlie as Gertrude, the queen
Jean Simmons as Ophelia, daughter of Polonius
Rating: 💀💀💀💀💀

Brilliantly reduced. Olivier announces right at the beginning, "This is the story of a man who couldn't make up his mind." Well! Hardly worth sticking around to see the rest, is it? It's said that an actor has two choices playing Hamlet: He can be a "to be" Hamlet, or a "not to be" Hamlet. Olivier's a "not to be." Every generation gets its own melancholy Dane: If you like yours really oversimplified, this is the *Hamlet* for you.

---

[75] ". . . tragical-historical, tragical-comical-historical-pastoral, scene individable, or poem unlimited." *Hamlet*, Act II, Scene 2: Polonius rambling on, as usual.
[76] Well, okay, there's a *ghost*.

Hamlet (1964)
Directed by John Gielgud
Richard Burton as Hamlet
Alfred Drake as Claudius
Hume Cronyn as Polonius
Eileen Herlie as Gertrude
Rating: 🎭 🎭 🎭

If you think the only way to watch *Hamlet* is in the theater but there isn't a production happening nearby, then this is the *Hamlet* for you.

This is billed as a "TheatroFilm," a marketing genius's fancy name for setting up cameras in Broadway's Lunt-Fontanne Theater and filming an actual performance of John Gielgud's 1964 production of *Hamlet* starring Richard Burton, then at the height of his post-*Camelot*, post-*Cleopatra*, mid–Elizabeth Taylor paparazzi frenzy. It's not a great movie by any means, but it's a fascinating look at Gielgud's direction and Burton's approach to a great role. Gielgud conceived the production as a final pre-costume run-through. Accordingly, the actors wear rehearsal clothes: suits with swords, cocktail dresses with flowing muslin skirts, and early-sixties leisurewear like slacks and cardigans. The only scenery is a series of platforms, a large wooden door up center, and the large silhouette of Hamlet's father on the back wall (with the voice of director Gielgud playing the ghost). There's still visual interest, but the focus is really on terrific actors interpreting Shakespeare's play, all of whom tend to almost sing the dialogue, which is surely something they caught unconsciously from Gielgud (their voices are required to fill a Broadway house).

Burton's only interpretive choice is simply to be Richard Burton playing Hamlet, which, as it turns out, is a pretty good choice. Eileen Herlie reprises her Gertrude from Olivier's film, and Alfred Drake (who, among other things, played the original Curly in Broadway's *Oklahoma!*) is both a villainous and tormented Claudius, but Hume Cronyn is the standout: His is surely the funniest Polonius on film, which gives his death more emotional impact than in other versions. (Wait—we didn't just give away anything, did we?)

Still, grab some popcorn and pack a lunch: At three hours and eleven minutes this will take a while.

Hamlet (1990)
Directed by Franco Zeffirelli
Mel Gibson as Hamlet
Glenn Close as Gertrude
Alan Bates as Claudius
Ian Holm as Polonius
Helena Bonham Carter as Ophelia
Rating: 💀 💀 💀 💀

Mel Gibson apparently unknowingly auditioned for Hamlet when he played his own "To be or not to be" near-suicide scene (brilliantly) in *Lethal Weapon*. This is a classic, old-fashioned, movie-star version of the play, full of bright colors and famous actors, the kind of movie where the actress playing Hamlet's mother (Glenn Close) is only nine years older than her "son." Mel's a "to be" Hamlet for sure, especially when he puts his "antic disposition on." If you like your twenty-something Hamlet played by a thirty-something movie star, this is the *Hamlet* for you.

Hamlet (1996)
Directed by Kenneth Branagh
Written by William Shakespeare and Kenneth Branagh
Kenneth Branagh as Hamlet
Derek Jacobi as Claudius
Julie Christie as Gertrude
Kate Winslet as Ophelia
Billy Crystal as First Gravedigger
John Gielgud as Priam
Robin Williams as Osric
Rating: 💀 💀 💀

If you like your *Hamlet* intact (as 'twere), without a single word cut and lasting four hours, then this is the *Hamlet* for you. Branagh used all of it, combining the text of both the 1604 Second Quarto with the First Folio of 1623; for some reason this achievement was rewarded with an Academy Award nomination for Best Adapted Screenplay (it might have been a typo; maybe they meant *Least* Adapted Screenplay).

There's something perverse, it has to be said, about any production of a Shakespeare text that claims—with pride, yet—to be "complete and uncut." There's much disagreement over the various sources: Was every single word written by Shakespeare, or was some of it interpolated by the actors or "improved" by Folio editors Hemminges and Condell? Plus, you end up with a four-hour movie.

But Branagh, to his credit, puts it all out there and lets you decide. And he fills the cast with many of his Renaissance Theater regulars (Brian Blessed, Richard Briers, and so on) as well as surprising cameos by Jack Lemmon and Charlton Heston (well, not surprising anymore), and such unexpected Shakespeareans as Billy Crystal and Robin Williams. As in *Henry V*, he depicts several scenes that are only talked about in the play, adding a visual component to all the chatter; sometimes, with equal power, he lets the poetry just sing for itself. So it's a remarkable achievement.

But, did we mention it's four hours?

Hamlet (1990)
Directed by Kevin Kline
Kevin Kline as Hamlet
Dana Ivey as Gertrude
Brian Murray as Claudius
Josef Sommer as Polonius
Rating: 🖋️🖋️

If you like your filmed Shakespeare uncluttered by scenery or anything of visual interest, this is the *Hamlet* for you. This is a Broadway Archive video (available on DVD) of Kevin Kline's production at Joseph Papp's New York Shakespeare Festival. It's very simple, surprisingly complete, and a very smart reading of the text. It's just not very interesting as a *movie*.

This is the true "plank and a passion" version: Like Brooke Shields and her Calvins, nothing gets between the viewer and Shakespeare's words. Kline acts with his usual intelligence, wit, and passion (on top of everything else, the dude can cry on a dime), but still he doesn't really seem suited to the part of the melancholy Dane. Although he performs with the same gusto and energy he brought to the role of the Pirate King in *Pirates of Penzance* (another Public Theater/Kline triumph), and this performance is always interesting, we're just not sure it's *Hamlet*.

It's a marvelous record, though, and will have to suffice until the DVD for *Pirates of Penzance* comes out. Really—*The Pirates of Penzance*, man—that movie rocked.

THE COMPLETE WORKS OF WILLIAM SHAKESPEARE (abridged) *(2001)*

Directed by Paul Kafno
Written by Adam Long, Daniel Singer, and Jess Winfield
Additional Material by Reed Martin
Adam Long as Juliet, Ophelia, et al.
Reed Martin as Romeo, Polonius, et al.
Austin Tichenor as Hamlet, Macbeth, et al.
Rating: 💀 💀 💀 💀 💀

Co-author Austin Tichenor's performance as Hamlet on the DVD of the Reduced Shakespeare Company production on PBS must be considered definitive. It's the *only* filmed interpretation of Hamlet by a scholarly amateur who's in way over his head, and who appears for some reason to be channeling TV's Frasier Crane. It's mercifully brief; the shortest filmed *Hamlet* on record. For this relief, much thanks.

HAMLET *(2000)*

Directed by Michael Almereyda
Ethan Hawke as Hamlet
Kyle MacLachlan as Claudius
Sam Shepard as the Ghost
Diane Venora as Gertrude
Bill Murray as Polonius
Rating: 💀 💀 💀 💀 💀

We saved the best for last. This is a modern-dress version that's really quite extraordinary. Almereyda translates Shakespeare's text into the vocabulary of film with what seems like unnatural ease. He divides up the text, breaking up monologues into conversational chunks, often continuing a monologue through several changes of location and the passage of time. The acting is terrific across the board (with the disappointing exception of Bill Murray's Polonius), but the usually stoic Sam Shepard is a revelation as the Ghost, and Ethan Hawke really nails the melancholy Dane. If you like your Hamlet as a grieving disaffected college student (which, after all, is the character who Shakespeare actually wrote) played finally by an age-appropriate actor, then this is the *Hamlet* for you.

Movies Inspired by HAMLET

TO BE OR NOT TO BE (1942)
  Directed by Ernst Lubitsch
  Written by Edwin Justus Mayer
  Jack Benny as Joseph Tura
  Carole Lombard as Maria Tura
  Robert Stack as Lt. Stanislav Sobinski
  Rating: 💀 💀 💀 💀 💀

Jack Benny stars as the leader of a Polish theater company forced to join the anti-Nazi Underground. Obviously, it can't begin to reach the same artistic highs as *Hogan's Heroes* (how you feel about that is up to you), but it's a wonderfully funny drama . . . or, if you prefer, a wonderfully dramatic comedy. Jack Benny plays a ham Hamlet—"famous the world over in Poland"—whose wife (Carole Lombard) is having an affair in her dressing room during his interminable delivery of Hamlet's "To be or not to be" speech.

But when her lover (a dashing Polish pilot) discovers the identity of a Nazi spy who plans to destroy the Underground, husband and wife must reunite to *play the roles of their lives!*

Marketing hyperbole aside, though, it's really good. Carole Lombard was such a gifted actor and comedienne, and her death

---

[77] A line was cut from the movie after Lombard's death. When warned against meeting her lover in his plane, Lombard's character originally asked, "What can happen in a plane?"

after filming this movie (ironically, in a plane crash after returning from selling war bonds) was a great loss.[77] And Jack Benny was never better. Mel Brooks's 1983 remake is obviously more knowing about what the Nazis were actually up to, but it works harder, and less successfully, to sustain the sophisticated tone that the 1941 film manages so elegantly.

ROSENCRANTZ AND GUILDENSTERN ARE DEAD (1990)

Written and directed by Tom Stoppard (based on his play)
Gary Oldman as Rosencrantz
Tim Roth as Guildenstern
Richard Dreyfuss as the Player

Rating: 💀 💀

Everybody rise and give it up for Tom Stoppard. Not only did he re-energize the short-funny-alternative-Bard industry with *Dogg's Hamlet* (carrying on a time-honored tradition of satirizing Shakespeare begun by Ben Jonson and continued by W. S. Gilbert, Robert Benchley, and the Reduced Shakespeare Company, among others), he also helped Marc Norman write the delightful screenplay *Shakespeare in Love*, and he created *Rosencrantz and Guildenstern Are Dead*, his worm's-eye view of *Hamlet* in which Rosencrantz and Guildenstern (minor characters in Shakespeare's play) become the leading characters in their own story and discover they aren't up to the task. Filled with Stoppardian wit, Shakespearean in-jokes, and Beckettian existential dread, Stoppard examines a world in which "every exit is an entrance somewhere else."

So it's a bummer to report the movie's a bit of a drag. Although very funny in spots, and a treat to watch Gary Oldman play a bumbling, funny, nice guy, you can't avoid the fact that the play is ultimately about two guys who merely watch and wait. Action heroes they're not.

With that caveat, however—enjoy.

IN THE BLEAK MIDWINTER (1995)

Written and directed by Kenneth Branagh
Known in the United States as *A Midwinter's Tale*, this is a

charming little movie about a community theater production of *Hamlet*. As the marketing tagline says, "The Drama. The Passion. The Intrigue . . . and the rehearsals haven't even started." A Shakespearean *Waiting for Guffman*.

Rating: 💀 💀 💀

HENRY IV, PART 1
Filmed Versions: One
Notable Film Versions: Um, one
In the BBC version from 1979, Jon Finch (Polanski's Macbeth) plays King Henry, and Anthony Quayle's performance as Falstaff is sensational, we hear. There are also several versions of Luigi Pirandello's *Enrico IV*, which is not the same thing. Don't be fooled.

Movies Inspired by HENRY IV, PART 1

MY OWN PRIVATE IDAHO (1991)
Written and directed by Gus Van Sant
River Phoenix as Mike Waters
Keanu Reeves as Scott Favor
Rating: 💀 💀 💀
Remember the 1990s, when everybody was making volcano and virus movies? *My Own Private Idaho* was one of dozens of gay-narcoleptic-male-prostitutes-in-Oregon-based-on-Shakespeare movies. You couldn't *buy* an original idea back then.

Henry IV directly inspired *Idaho*, and director-writer Gus Van Sant borrows plot elements and language that he paraphrases and even quotes directly. But there are other Shakespearean echoes, as well: issues of class, friendship, loyalty, family; men acting as women (or at least taking traditionally female roles); and narcolepsy serving as a contemporary version of the sleeping potions used in every third Shakespeare play. And, like many of the thirty-nine plays, the settings jump around to many different international locations: Van Sant's not bound by the Aristotelian unities, you might say.[78]

---

[78] If you were way pretentious.

But, really, *My Own Private Idaho* is about the bonding of men, a frequent theme in Shakespeare's plays. It makes one long for Gus Van Sant to film *Othello*. Iago's love for the Moor would be a little less latent, a little mo' *blatant*, naw'mean?

CHIMES AT MIDNIGHT (1967)

This is Orson Welles's crowning Shakespearean achievement, in which he brings a robust magnificence to Falstaff, Shakespeare's greatest comic creation and a part Welles was born to play. He had a brilliant idea: Create a story that focused on Falstaff by taking the relevant scenes from all the plays in which Falstaff appears (*Henry VI, Parts 1* and *2, Henry V, Richard II,* and *The Merry Wives of Windsor*). He even used Holinshed's *Chronicles* (Shakespeare's own original source) for the narration. Welles's performance is outstanding, and the battle scenes are impressively intense.

Unfortunately, crowning achievement or not, Welles's glory days as a director were far behind him. It's too bad he wouldn't trust the production to a director who could obtain some strong studio support. There are so many technical glitches that it becomes impossible to follow the story, and Welles had two incredibly distracting directorial habits: He seems to always put the camera in a hole in the floor (so you watch the actors' chins against a backdrop of sky), and he loved the sights and sounds of background actors laughing. It's even more annoying than listening to a laugh track on a sitcom: this way, you're *watching* it, too. Welles seemed to forget that when you want an audience to cry, you don't let the actor cry. It's the same when you want the audience to laugh. Sigh. Very disappointing.

Rating: 💀

HENRY IV, PART 2
Film Versions: One
Notable Film Versions: Only the BBC version, although the animated classic *Scooby-Doo Meets the Harlem Globetrotters* shares the same sense of youthful indiscretion giving way to adult responsibility. But that could be the merlot talking.

HENRY V
Film Versions: Nine
Notable Film versions: Two

Henry V (1944)
Directed by Laurence Olivier
Laurence Olivier as King Henry V
Rating: 💀 💀 💀

Henry V (1989)
Directed by Kenneth Branagh
Derek Jacobi as Chorus
Kenneth Branagh as King Henry V
Ian Holm as Fluellen
Judi Dench as Mistress Quickly
Robbie Coltrane as Falstaff
Emma Thompson as Katherine
Rating: 💀 💀 💀 💀

These two films were made in very different times for very different reasons. Olivier reportedly was asked by Winston Churchill to make *Henry V* as propaganda, hoping it would inspire the English people to support an invasion of France in World War II. Accordingly, Olivier eliminated scenes that showed doubt or unpleasant consequences (again, reportedly at Churchill's request), and the final victorious Battle of Agincourt (filmed in Ireland over a six-week period) is indeed thrilling.

Branagh, on the other hand, was interested in the struggles of men in power, the decisions they must make, the relationships they must compromise, and their reflective moments as they deal with matters of state and order men to go to war. (Branagh had a private three-hour interview with Prince Charles, who provided royal insight and was much taken with Branagh's interpretation of the role when he saw him perform it live in Stratford.) Branagh's Battle of Agincourt is a much bloodier, muddier business than Olivier's (Branagh's *entire movie* was shot in only seven weeks) and while it's still thrilling in an action-movie kind of way, it's a more sober experience.

Both versions are terrific, in their own ways, even though Branagh's has the edge. And both movies end with English victories over France, which made them crowd-pleasing hits in England. Really, pummeling France: What's not to like?

HENRY VI, PART 1
Film Versions: One
Notable Film Versions: One
Directed by Jane Howell (1983)

The BBC series finally gets a doozy here—the *only* filmed or taped version of the three parts of Shakespeare plays about Henry VI, featuring strong performances from some fine actors you've never heard of, including future Academy Award nominee (*Secrets and Lies*) and BAFTA winner Brenda Blethyn, as well as future *Titanic* captain and Middle Earth ruler Bernard Hill. We think if you watch it, you'll come away with the same feelings we had: boredom, nausea, and fatigue.

Rating: 💀💀

FUN FACT: In England, the name Bernard is pronounced with the accent on the first syllable. In America, the name Bernard is pronounced with the accent on the second syllable. In both countries, boys named Bernard get beat up a lot.

HENRY VI, PART 2
Film Versions: One
Notable Film Versions: One

The standout here is the Reduced Shakespeare Company's *The Complete Works of William Shakespeare (abridged)* (available on DVD). In its section devoted to the History plays, the RSC divides the actual King Henry VI himself into three parts.

Don't blink or you'll miss it: The middle part lasts no more than a fraction of a second, which some scholars maintain is still a fraction of a second more than the play is worth.

Rating: 💀 💀 💀 💀 💀

Shameless Self-Promotion

FUN FACT: Did you know you can buy Reduced Shakespeare Company DVDs (as well as their near-legendary stage scripts and mildly humorous recordings) at www. reducedshakespeare.com?

HENRY VI, PART 3
Film Versions: One
Notable Film Versions: One

Here, attention must be paid to *Carry On Henry*, one of the standouts of the British *Carry On* films, a series of broad, bawdy comedies that often dealt with historic subjects and featured Britain's leading comic actors of the day.[79] *Carry On Henry*, is about Henry VIII, not Henry VI, but we have plenty of Henry VIII films to talk about and no films about Henry VI to talk about. Give us a break.

Rating: 💀 💀 💀

HENRY VIII
Film Versions Listed: Eleven
Notable Film Versions: Three

We're going to fudge here and include two films about Henry VIII that aren't based on Shakespeare's play. Why? Because they're too good, and it's our book.

The Private Life of Henry VIII is the 1933 film starring Charles Laughton that gives us the popular image we have of Henry as a loud, boisterous, belching sybarite who gnaws on turkey legs and tosses the bones over his shoulder. Laughton's performance must

---

[79] And some American comic actors: Co-author Reed Martin can be seen in almost all of his glory performing the role of Pocahontas in *Carry On Columbus*. This was also the final film in the series. Coincidence? You decide.

Fig. 20. The six wives of Henry VIII: Anne Boleyn, Jane Seymour, uh . . . damn. Let's just say Moe, Larry, Curly, and Shemp.

be considered definitive even if most scholars believe it's not historically accurate (in that sense, just like Shakespeare's play). And the title is meant (we think) to be ironic, for surely no king of England has ever had such a public "private life," with the possible exception of the future King Charles (or his son, King William).

Rating: 💀💀💀

The Six Wives of Henry VIII is the 1971 television miniseries that was hugely popular in both England and (as part of PBS's *Masterpiece Theater*) in America. Yes, it was pure soap opera, but it corrected some of the historical inaccuracies from the 1933 film. And yes, it's television, but we're not snobs.

Rating: 💀💀💀💀

Finally, there's the 1979 BBC version of the play—and, seriously, what would we do without the BBC? If it weren't for them, we'd have no filmed record of many of Shakespeare's works. Sure, most of the BBC versions stink: They apparently thought that just getting great English actors in a studio and turning on a camera without plausible scenery or any kind of overall directorial vision would be enough. It isn't. But at least they exist, that's what's important. And their *Henry VIII* is one of the standouts of the series.[80]

JULIUS CAESAR
> **Film Versions: Seventeen**
> **Notable Film Versions: One**
> Directed by Joseph L. Mankiewicz (1953)
> Marlon Brando as Marc Antony

---

[80] No, of course we didn't watch it. Standout or no, it's still *Henry VIII*, a tough slog at the best of times, and because there are only so many hours in the day, we'd really much prefer to watch the *Taming of the Shrew* teen-comedy-knockoff *10 Things I Hate About You* (see page 212). Priorities, people. It's all about establishing priorities.

James Mason as Brutus

John Gielgud as Cassius

This was the all-star Hollywood version that settled once and for all whether American-style Method acting (as personified by Marlon Brando at his height, if not his weight) could compete with great British actors performing Shakespeare.

It can't.

On the other hand, where else do you get to see Marlon Brando and John Gielgud perform together? Nowhere, that's where. And for good reason.

Rating: 💀 💀 💀

KING JOHN

FilmVersions: Three

Notable Film Versions: Three

In 1899, the great nineteenth-century actor Sir Herbert Beerbohm Tree directed himself in what was the very first film adaptation of Shakespeare. It's a rare record of nineteenth-century acting styles, and there's another reason to celebrate: It's only three minutes long! Outstanding.

Rating: 💀 💀 💀 (one per minute)

The second notable film version of *King John* is *any* version of Robin Hood (except Kevin Costner's). Even the animated Disney version includes a derogatory folk song about Prince John (since Richard was still technically the monarch, John hadn't yet been elected king) that features the lines,"Too late to be known as John the First / He's sure to be known as John the Worst." This is more historical accuracy than even Shakespeare attempted.

Rating: 💀 💀 💀

Honorable mention also has to go to *The Lion in Winter* (either the 1968 version with Peter O'Toole and Katharine Hepburn or the 2003 Patrick Stewart/Glenn Close version), which features not-yet-Prince John in a supporting role. It's ancient history as contemporary domestic drama, with Henry II and his wife Katherine of Aragon squabbling over their four sons: Henry (who's dead), Richard (not yet the Lionheart), John (an overweight daddy's boy), and Geoffrey (this family's Zeppo.) It's a literate and funny script, and either movie will give you the feeling of watching Shakespeare without *actually* watching Shakespeare, which is a special added bonus.

Rating: 💀 💀 💀 💀.

KING LEAR

FilmVersions: 15
Notable Film Versions: One
RAN (1985)
Directed by Akira Kurosawa

Lear has been played on film by Ian Holm, Brian Blessed, Michael Hordern (twice), James Earl Jones, Patrick Magee, Paul Scofield, Patrick Stewart (in the made-for-TV Western adaptation, *King of Texas*), Orson Welles, and (inevitably) Laurence Olivier. It's one of those roles, epic and challenging, that actors of a certain age can't wait to attempt. Trouble is, when an actor gets old enough to fully plumb the depths of the character, he's not strong enough to lift Cordelia at the end. So that's fun.

Despite the number of great actors who've played the role (almost all of whom are worth a look), the one adaptation of *Lear* that's made any kind of real impact on the public is Akira Kurosawa's *Ran*, set in ancient feudal Japan. It's visually magnificent, and to hear Shakespeare spoken in the original Japanese is a rare treat.

Rating: 💀 💀 💀 💀 💀

Movies Inspired by KING LEAR

THE DRESSER (1981)

Directed by Peter Yates
Written by Ronald Harwood (based on his play)
Albert Finney as Sir
Tom Courtenay as Norman

A funny and touching portrait of a grand theatrical ham and his loyal dresser, this is a great depiction of a touring Shakespeare company in World War II–era England. The backstage squabbling, the transportation issues ("Stop! That! Train!" thunders

Albert Finney), the insecurities, the jealousies, the futility, and ultimately the rewards—one can imagine this story being true no matter what the era. And if the opinion of a former nonactress girlfriend is any indication, the movie's equally enjoyable for people who aren't theater folk.

Rating: 🖤🖤🖤🖤.

A THOUSAND ACRES (1997)

Based on Jane Smiley's book: *Lear* on an Iowa farm.

Rating: 🖤🖤

CHARLIE'S ANGELS (2000)

Charlie is Lear, the Angels are his daughters, Bosley's the Fool. Think about it.

Rating: 🖤🖤🖤🖤🖤

LOVE'S LABOUR'S LOST

FilmVersions: Four
Notable Film Versions: One
Written and directed by Kenneth Branagh (2000)
Kenneth Branagh as Berowne
Alicia Silverstone as the Princess of France
Natascha McElhone as Rosaline
Timothy Spall as Don Armado
Nathan Lane as Costard

Rating: 🖤🖤🖤

None of the faithful adaptations can breathe much life into this dated and not very lively play, but Branagh's fun musical version comes close. Co-produced by *Singin' in the Rain* director Stanley Donen and set in the late 1930s, as war in Europe was looming, Branagh adds big 1950s-style musical dance numbers, shoots them like honest-to-goodness M-G-M extravaganzas from Hollywood's glory days, and finds modern equivalents to Shakespeare's poetry in the songs of Cole Porter, Irving Berlin, and George and Ira Gershwin. It's fun to watch Branagh and company (including, in this case, the guy who plays Shaggy in the *Scooby-Doo* movies) sing and dance (hey, we also loved Lee

Marvin and Clint Eastwood singing in *Paint Your Wagon*). He even retains many of Shakespeare's rhyming couplets. Problem is he retains *too* many, and at ninety-four minutes the movie still feels at least ten minutes too long.

Shakespeare's ridiculous plot about men foreswearing women in favor of study seems ideal source material for a silly musical, but it just ain't enough. Ah well, it's not Branagh's fault. The kid's talented, but he's not a miracle worker.

MACBETH
> **Film Versions: Over forty**
> **Notable Film Versions: One**

> *Macbeth* (1969)
> Directed by Roman Polanski
> Jon Finch as Macbeth
> Francesca Annis as Lady Macbeth
> Martin Shaw as Banquo
> **Rating:** 💀💀💀💀

This will stand for a very long time as the definitive filmed *Macbeth*. Its grim realism, the mark of a master director who was working in the shadows of his own personal tragedies, makes it seem, thirty-five years after its initial release, as if it were filmed yesterday. Jon Finch's title performance is haunting and entirely convincing as a dutiful soldier who gradually rises to ambitious tyranny. Interestingly, in contrast to other versions, he's not depicted as henpecked. If anything, Lady Macbeth is swept up by her husband's ambition, and Francesca Annis portrays her love, her cooperation, and her descent into madness in all its frightening depth.

The brutality of the violence can be off-putting, but it sure doesn't seem gratuitous. It seems perfectly true to ancient Scotland and, sadly, more recent times. You can't help remembering that director Roman Polanski's wife Sharon Tate had been brutally murdered earlier in 1969, before he started filming. And Polanski has said he based the scene where Macbeth's men massacre Macduff's family on his childhood memories of SS troops ransacking his house in Poland.

Notorious when it was released because it was produced by *Playboy* magazine, the movie will disappoint those only looking for Shakespearean boobies. They're there, all right, but only on the ancient midnight hags: there's nothing (you'll pardon the expression) titillating here at all.

Movies based on MACBETH

THRONE OF BLOOD (1957)

Akira Kurosawa's samurai version. Very stylized. Very spooky. Very cool.

Rating:

MEN OF RESPECT (1991)

Written and Directed by William Reilly
John Turturro as Mike Battaglia
Katherine Borowitz as Ruthie Battaglia
Dennis Farina as Bankie Como
Peter Boyle as Matt Duffy

A 1991 Mafia version, giving credit to Shakespeare as its source and turning Macbeth into Mike Battaglia, a brutally insecure and ambitious Mafia goon. It's great to see John Turturro tear into his role of Macbeth/Mikey B; Dennis Farina, Peter Boyle, and Stanley Tucci bring credit to their cleverly named Macbeth surrogates; and thematically, the song remains the same: *There's no honor among thieves* (or, *Be careful what you wish for*. Take your pick).

But several things keep the movie from being great. Katherine Borowitz is no match for Turturro as his onscreen wife, many of the supporting cast aren't very convincing, and the soundtrack is homemade porn-movie bad. But, most important, by making *Men of Respect* a faithful transliteration of Macbeth's plot points, the movie never becomes its own thing. It's *Macbeth*, for sure, but *The Godfather* and *The Sopranos* feel more richly Shakespearean. There's more humanity in those violent Mafia epics: more wit, more depth, more doomed ambition, and a greater sense of twisted, haunted grandeur. Okay, okay, maybe that's too much weight to put on Shakespeare's shortest little tragedy, but watching this modern updating brings it out. On the other hand, John Turturro gets to yell "Not a man o' woman born can do shit ta me!" So it's not a total loss.

Rating: 🕱

JOE MACBETH (1953)

Another gangster version. Rent *The Sopranos* instead.

Rating: 🕱

SCOTLAND, PA (2002)

Written and directed by Billy Morrissette
James LeGros as Joe "Mac" McBeth
Maura Tierney as Pat McBeth
Christopher Walken as Lieutenant McDuff

In terms of modern updatings, we prefer this surprisingly faithful translation that sets Shakespeare's familiar story amid the cutthroat world of 1970s fast-food restaurants. As that description suggests, this adaptation accentuates the plot's absurdities and highlights the comedy without losing the grim repercussions of lust and ambition. James LeGros and *ER*'s Maura Tierney are funny, haunting, and sympathetic as Joe "Mac" McBeth and his wife, Pat,[81] and Christopher Walken has a ball as the suspicious detective McDuff (with honorable mention going to John Cariani as his Barney Fife-ish deputy).

Added bonus? The soundtrack rocks to the music of Bad Company (who recorded the haunting-in-this-context "Bad Company," "Feel Like Makin' Love," and other 1970s classics). Shakespeare may have been a genius, but Bad Company he was not.

Rating: 🕱 🕱 🕱 🕱

MEASURE FOR MEASURE
Film Versions: Two
Notable Film Versions: None

---

[81] Incredible but true: The plaid oven mitt that Pat uses to cover up the burn on her hand is the tartan pattern from the actual Macbeth clan.

THE MERCHANT OF VENICE
  Film Versions: Around twenty
  Notable Film Versions: Two

The MERCHANT OF *Venice* (2001)
Directed by Trevor Nunn
Henry Goodman as Shylock
David Bamber as Antonio
Alexander Hanson as Bassanio
Derbhle Crotty as Portia
Rating: 💀💀

The Merchant of Venice (2004)
Directed by Michael Radford
Al Pacino as Shylock
Jeremy Irons as Antonio
Joseph Fiennes as Bassanio
Lynne Collins as Portia
Rating: 💀

Shakespeare's comedies are tricky buggers. It's so difficult to get the tone right. If you play them too broadly, you risk losing the humanity of the characters and the empathy of the audience. But if you play them too realistically, it becomes impossible to accept the ridiculous turns of plot.

Which brings us, sadly, to *The Merchant of Venice*.

As we mentioned in our discussion of *Hamlet*, one of the measures of a play's greatness is how well it can hold up to repeated viewings. By this standard, our opinion of *Merchant* fell faster than a clown's pants on gag night.

Trevor Nunn's *Merchant* starts off quite promisingly, with Jazz-Age music accompanying old film clips of Venetian society circa 1930. It's an ingenious use of film technique to set the tone, and you sit back, relaxed with the assurance that Shakespeare's problematic comedy will be handled with a light touch.

Alas, that feeling lasts only as long as the opening credits. Then the story begins, and you see it's being shot on tape in a TV studio. Your heart sinks. It sinks a little more when Antonio starts sighing theatrically and acting between the lines, not on them. And you think, " *Oy*, this is gonna take a while."

But you can't fault the actors: they approach the material truthfully and invest it with all the craft at their command. The fault, dear reader, is with the director—and the playwright. Shakespeare, after all, is the one who assembled all these incompatible elements, and rather than excuse them, director Nunn encouraged a level of emotional commitment from his actors that requires us, the audience, to take the characters as seriously as they do. Problem is, if we do that, we have to start asking serious questions.

What's with all the casket nonsense? Why does Portia play the home version of *Let's Make a Deal* to choose a husband? Why does Antonio accept Shylock's ridiculous bargain (a loan of 3,000 ducats versus a pound of flesh if he defaults)? Why would the judge accept the "certification" of the unknown stranger "Balthazar" in a capital case? What, in her background, training, or education gives Portia the idea and (you'll pardon the expression) the *balls* to dress up as a man and give expert testimony? Why does nobody recognize her? Why is she the smartest legal mind in the courtroom? Why, after her eloquent plea about "the quality of mercy," does she then insist on a punishment so lacking in mercy that it's positively medieval? And why, after she's been so cold-hearted to Shylock and tricked her husband into giving up the ring she only recently presented to him, are we supposed to give a damn about her hurt feelings?

We submit that *these* are the real reasons the play's considered "problematic," not because of its alleged anti-Semitism. Shylock's behavior is for the most part completely understandable (if indefensible), partly because Henry Goodman's performance is so strong, and because Nunn successfully points up the differences in class, adds several passages in Hebrew, and doesn't shy away from the play's depiction of anti-Semitism. You feel Shylock's outrage at being ill used and his pain at the loss of his daughter.

Then there's the big-budget, widescreen, Al Pacino version. It's magnificent to look at; if only Trevor Nunn had had Radford's budget and had been allowed to shoot in Venice. Jeremy Irons anchors the movie, and Al Pacino divests himself of many of his most annoying mannerisms but, perhaps burdened by his fame and familiarity, remains "Al Pacino," never really becoming Shylock. And Lynne Collins is very strong but can't overcome Shakespeare's problem that the two different Portias are almost from two different plays. Shots of her consulting with an elderly lawyer help her courtroom appearance make a little more sense, but only a little.

Radford dramatizes some of the incidents only mentioned in Shakespeare's play (Bassanio spitting on Shylock, for instance) but the sense that the Venetian Jews constitute a separate and distinct community of "others" is stronger in Nunn's version. Radford also tries to soft-peddle the anti-Semitic rhetoric in the courtroom. The actors almost seem to apologize for the words they're forced to say, but it doesn't help: The characters' actions are still hateful.

Finally, however, after all these viewings, we ultimately admire Shakespeare's depiction of Shylock. He could have made Shylock a saint, an upstanding paragon of morality. But no, Shakespeare has enough respect for the character to make Shylock as much of a selfish prick as all his other distasteful characters, which in its day was a groundbreaking achievement. Today, *The Merchant of Venice* shouldn't be considered an anti-Semitic play, just a bad one.

ESSAY QUESTION: *Are we wrong? Is* Merchant *really as good as everybody says? If you think it is, discuss the ways in which you are not a brainwashed pod-person.*

Another notable *MERCHANT*:
THE MAORI MERCHANT OF VENICE (2002)
From New Zealand, the first film shot entirely in the Maori language.
Rating: 🎭🎭🎭🎭🎭
(Oh, who are we kidding? We havent seen it.)

THE MERRY WIVES OF WINDSOR
Film Versions: Nine
Notable Film Versions: None

Not even the sterling cast of Richard Griffiths (Harry Potter's uncle Vernon Dursley) as Falstaff, plus Prunella Scales (Sybil Fawlty from *Fawlty Towers*) and Judy Davis as the two scheming mistresses can turn the BBC version into anything worth watching.

A MIDSUMMER NIGHT'S DREAM
Film Versions: Twenty
Notable Film Versions: Three

A Midsummer Night's Dream (1935)
Directed by Max Reinhardt and William Dieterle
James Cagney as Bottom, the Weaver
Joe E. Brown as Flute, the Bellows-Mender
Dick Powell as Lysander, in love with Hermia
Mickey Rooney as Puck, or Robin Goodfellow, a Fairy
Olivia De Havilland as Hermia
Rating:

The great M-G-M studio used to boast that it had "More Stars Than There Are in Heaven!" Well, this was Warner Bros., not M-G-M, and not even all of Hollywood's greatest stars (at the time) couldn't make this into anything but a train wreck. Mickey Rooney couldn't be more annoying, and even the great Jimmy Cagney seems in over his head.

A Midsummer Night's Dream (1968)
Directed by Peter Hall
David Warner as Lysander
Diana Rigg as Helena
Helen Mirren as Hermia
Paul Rogers as Bottom
Ian Richardson as Oberon
Judi Dench as Titania
Ian Holm as Puck

Rating: 🗿🗿

The DVD of this film is a mess: scratchy, unsynced sound, white titles you can't read because they bleed into white backgrounds, scenes that skip like an old record. We can't imagine it played like this on its original release: It's like watching an old print that got walked on by somebody wearing golf cleats.

But if you can get past the technical glitches, this version is an odd but fun trip down memory lane, and a wonderful way to see some great English actors in their youth (and some in the buff). Director Peter Hall was clearly inspired by Richard Lester's (superior) direction of *A Hard Day's Night*; like Lester he uses jump cuts, fast motion, characters (the fairies) disappearing in and out of frame, actors glancing conspiratorially at the camera. Diana Rigg and Helen Mirren play the young female lovers with the kind of exaggerated truth that allows you to believe and sympathize with them, but also to laugh. David Warner's Lysander looks like this whole thing is beneath him; a reason, we believe, that this terrific actor's movie career mostly consists of playing bad guys. And the pre-damed Judi Dench is wonderful as the mostly topless Titania.

Unfortunately, Peter Hall directs his actors (at least in the several productions of his that we've seen) to behave not as real people but only as stiff actors, standing and saying the lines, letting the verse do the work. Great, but a little quirky human behavior's nice, too. Rigg and Mirren escape this limitation and give lively performances, and in an odd way, the most realistic and detailed performance might be Ian Holm's antic, snake-tongued performance as Puck.

A Midsummer Night's Dream (1999)
Directed by Michael Hoffman
Kevin Kline as Bottom
Michelle Pfeiffer as Titania
Rupert Everett as Oberon
Stanley Tucci as Puck
Calista Flockhart as Hermia

Anna Friel as Helena
Christian Bale as Demetrius
Dominic West as Lysander
Roger Rees as Peter Quince
Sam Rockwell as Snug/Thisby
Bill Irwin, Max Wright, and Gregory Jbara as Mechanicals
Rating: 💀 💀 💀 💀 💀

This is the best movie version of *Dream* out there. It's two-thirds terrific.

Despite it being written in five acts, *Dream* has always felt like it's more easily divided into three sections: the city, the forest, and the mechanicals. The weakest third in this case is the first: The actors playing the lovers do so a little too realistically, guided by a director who forgets that *Dream* is a comedy (it's a running gripe with us that the lovers should be just as funny as the mechanicals). The setting has been updated to an Edwardian Italian villa that's so rustic and countrified it eliminates completely any distinction between the repression of the city and the liberating freedom of the forest that's one of the main themes of the play. And urban society seems very sophisticated and civilized, except for the father demanding the death penalty for his daughter because she won't marry the man of his choosing. So that's weird.

But let's talk about what the movie gets right. Kevin Kline is in his element as Bottom, bringing grand theatricality and simple humanity to his role as the egomaniacal ass who actually becomes one. The so-called "rude mechanicals" are very funny, playing them realistically as earnest amateurs rather than as sophisticated clowns, and Sam Rockwell as Snug the joiner plays Thisby's final sorrowful speech wonderfully straight, surprising himself, his fellow players, his on-screen audience, and us.

And the fairies are perfect: *exactly* the way they behave in real life. The actors obviously studied actual fairies: Michelle Pfeiffer plays Titania with almost documentary verisimilitude. Eerie. And while Stanley Tucci's Puck is not as antic and chaos-loving as Ian Holm's was, he might be the slyest and most endearing. (One word of warning, though: Rupert Everett mumbles the part of Oberon like a fairy Marlon Brando: You'll want at least a 7.1

home theater sound system cranked up to eleven to hear his lines.)

Fairies, sprites, nymphs, and satyrs haven't been portrayed this realistically on-screen ever. Clearly, they're making great strides in petitioning Hollywood to have their world presented on film with respect and dignity.

Movies Inspired by A MIDSUMMER NIGHT'S DREAM

A MIDSUMMER NIGHT'S RAVE (2002)

Never heard of it? Neither had we. It can't properly be labeled a disappointment, because our expectations weren't high. But at least in this version, the lovers are distinctly detailed characterizations: Xander (from Shakespeare's Lysander) has asthma, Damon (from Demetrius, we guess) has two earrings, Mia (Hermia) is blonde, and Elena (Helena) is brunette! See, you can *totally* tell them apart! O, what an exquisitely rich tapestry writer Robert Raymond and director Gil Cates Jr. weave from Shakespeare's original! If that weren't enough, Puck is part drug dealer/part queeny sidekick to OB John (*Get it?* It's Oberon!), who distributes a love drug to the ravers and flies in to save the lovers like a *deus ex Puckina*. All this and a techno soundtrack, too. And did we mention the hit man? Really, aside from the terrible writing, inexperienced direction, and mediocre acting, it doesn't get any better than this.

Rating: 💀

ESSAY QUESTION: *What's the difference between techno and disco? Seriously.*

A MIDSUMMER NIGHT'S SEX COMEDY (1982)

Director Woody Allen combines spoofs of Shakespeare and Ingmar Bergman's *Smiles of a Summer Night* to create this disappointing "Midsummer Night's Talkathon." He convincingly celebrates the countryside in much the way he celebrates Manhattan in many of his other movies, and the moments when he invokes the spirit world manage to be both funny and slightly eerie. But alas, three things sink this movie: The endless debate about art, love, intellect, and passion is entirely reflective and not very active; there's only a little sex; and there's even less comedy.

Rating: 💀

FUN FACT: The famous "Wedding March," to which millions of people have walked down the aisle, was written by Felix Mendelssohn in 1826 to accompany a live stage performance of *Dream*. It's featured in both the 1935 Max Reinhardt film version, and in Woody Allen's affectionate (but not very funny) spoof.

MUCH ADO ABOUT NOTHING
Film Versions: Ten
Notable Film Versions: One

Much Ado About Nothing (1993)
Directed by Kenneth Branagh
Kenneth Branagh as Benedick
Emma Thompson as Beatrice
Denzel Washington as Don Pedro of Aragon
Keanu Reeves as Don John
Michael Keaton as Constable Dogberry

Kenneth Branagh doesn't just film Shakespeare's plays, he turns them into *movies*, thoroughly designed and conceived to succeed on their own merits without relying on an audience's familiarity with the source material. As he said when he made *Henry V*, "I wanted to make a popular film that would satisfy the Shakespearean scholar as well as the filmgoers who like '*Crocodile' Dundee*." (In his defense, he said it a long time ago.[82]) And that's what he's done with *Much Ado*: He's made a bright, sun-dappled comedy with lots of laughs, romance, drama, and great, well-spoken poetry.

Oh, sure, you could quibble that at times the actors look like they're sitting around having too much fun vacationing in Italy instead of acting out the story; that the movie doesn't really get

---

[82] For a scholarly exegesis of the *"Crocodile" Dundee* oeuvre, see another book.

going until Keanu Reeves starts acting (brilliantly) like the bad guy; that the constable's horse-riding bit is stolen (sorry, *borrowed*) from *Monty Python and the Holy Grail*; and that Michael Keaton is working *much* harder than he needs to as Dogberry (with teeth yellowed from so much scenery-chewing).

But such quibbles are mean-spirited and Grinch-ish. Branagh and Emma Thompson speak the speeches as trippingly as if they speak in verse every day around the house. The cast includes big-time movie stars who headline their own movies (Denzel, Keanu, Keaton) and all do great ensemble work here, as well as the team of actors we've come to refer to as the Ken Branagh Dancers: Brian Blessed, Richard Briers, Jimmy Yuill, and composer Patrick Doyle.

Try as he might, however, even Branagh can't answer one of the most nagging questions in the Shakespearean canon: Why is it always the *priest* who comes up with an outlandish plot to deceive people into thinking someone else is dead?

Rating: 💀💀💀

ESSAY QUESTION: *Yeah, why is it always the priest who comes up with an outlandish plot to deceive people into thinking someone else is dead?*

OTHELLO
Film Versions: Twenty-eight
Notable Film Versions: Four

Othello (1952)
Directed by Orson Welles
Starring Orson Welles as Othello
Michael MacLiammoir as Iago
Suzanne Cloutier as Desdemona

Othello is the most storied of Welles's forays into filming Shakespeare. With no financial backing, he contrived to make his film a snippet at a time, reassembling his actors whenever he'd raised enough money to shoot another scene or two. He'd call them up with the news: Hey, I got some more money, meet me in

Spain for Act III, Scene 2! At one point, the costumes got lost on a train, so Welles simply filmed Roderigo's murder scene in a bathhouse. The result, with a towel-clad Iago stalking Roderigo, is inspired. It's a beautiful film.

Unfortunately, it's also mostly unwatchable. Since Welles couldn't afford adequate production values, he frequently recorded the soundtrack afterward in a studio. He then would simply pick the best sound take, whether it matched the visual or not, and plunk it in. The result is difficult to watch and almost impossible to follow. If you already know the story, though, it's a pleasure to watch Welles's imaginative use of shadow, water, and wind to visually underscore the poetry. And his simple, understated, one-shot performance of Othello's "courtship" speech is a testament to the power of an actor trusting the language. Moment to moment? Brilliant. Overall? Disaster.

Rating: 💀

Othello (1965)
Directed by Stuart Burge
Laurence Olivier as Othello
Maggie Smith as Desdemona
Frank Finlay as Iago

Regarded by many as the finest film adaptation of *Othello*, it's frustratingly hard to find. Olivier resisted playing the role, finally acquiesced, and toured it around Europe before committing it to film. He reportedly worked with weights to broaden his chest and expand his lung capacity so that he could develop his own reedy baritone into a glorious basso profundo. Alas, he's still a white guy playing a black guy, but seek it out if you can. With Frank Finlay reportedly stealing the movie from Olivier, Derek Jacobi, and a pre–Harry Potter Maggie Smith, you won't be disappointed.

Rating: 💀💀 (Based on its cast and reputation. Did we mention how tough it is to find?)

Othello (1995)
Directed by Oliver Parker
Laurence Fishburne as Othello

Kenneth Branagh as Iago
Irène Jacob as Desdemona
Rating: 💀 💀 💀

Like Richard III, Iago is one of Shakespeare's greatest villains and, like another Shakespearean hero, Ferris Bueller, speaks directly to the camera, confesses his evil deeds, shares his nefarious plans, and (more important) woos us over to his side, making the audience sympathetic co-conspirators.

Kenneth Branagh does this brilliantly as Iago in Oliver Parker's film version of *Othello*. Othello trusts Iago implicitly. Unfortunately, the scheming Iago hates him and convinces Othello that his faithful wife, Desdemona, has had an affair. We immediately believe Branagh as the jealous and bitter Iago. He has every reason to be jealous and bitter, seeing as how Emma Thompson won the Oscar that Branagh so coveted, and then dumped him.[83]

Laurence Fishburne portrays Othello. For some reason, he's the first black actor to play this role on film (what century are we in, people?). Fueled by Iago's lies and innuendo, Othello is driven to fits of jealousy and violence, and generally becomes a bad mother-fornicator; an Elizabethan Ike Turner.

Fishburne's Othello is powerful and sexy. From the bald head to the unplaceable accent, Fishburne has clearly based his performance on Yul Brynner's in *The Magnificent Seven*. In fact, you half expect him to start singing "Shall We Dance?" from *The King and I*. Alert viewers will also notice that the actor playing Cassio looks exactly like Brynner's co-star James Brolin in *Westworld*. Coincidence? You decide.

The film is most successful at dramatizing Othello's tragic flaw: his all-consuming jealousy. When possessed by the green-eyed monster, Fishburne twitches, shakes, and shudders as if he's either nobly enduring the fires of Hell or has just eaten some bad clams.

Comparisons have frequently been made between Othello and O. J. Simpson, but the textual evidence shows there's not much connection. Othello admits killing his wife, kills himself in

---

[83] Or was it the other way around? We're never quite sure who dumped who.

despair, and is not in the Football Hall of Fame. On the other hand, O.J. won the Heisman Trophy, was found not guilty, and has never portrayed Ike Turner. In fairness, though, it should be noted that both Othello and O.J. escaped via White Broncos.

Purists moan that director Oliver Parker jettisoned more than 70 percent of Shakespeare's text, and that Ian McKellen did the same in his screen adaptation of *Richard III*. This kind of reduction we heartily endorse. Make them *movies*, not museum pieces. Kenneth Branagh (probably in an Iago-like fit of jealous revenge) filmed *Hamlet* and didn't cut a single line, making a movie that's *four hours long*. Talk about tragic. (See our glowing review, page 174.)

Movies Based on OTHELLO

O (2001)

Written and directed by Tim Blake Nelson
Mekhi Phifer as Odin James
Julia Stiles as Desi
Josh Hartnett as Hugo
Andrew Keegan as Mike Cassio
Martin Sheen as Coach Duke
Rating: 💀 💀 💀

Here's the thing about tragedies: If you like them, you revel in the inescapable inevitability with which the characters reach their doomed fates. If you're not that impressed and believe that human beings have a divinely inspired thing called "free will," then you shake your head, mystified at the characters' inability to make an original choice, and tap your foot impatiently, waiting for the pieces to fall into place and the tragic destinies to claim their victims. Shakespeare's language makes up for a lot, but what happens if you take that away?

This question gets answered watching O, a modern retelling of Othello. It's a very solid, nicely conceived version of Shakespeare's play: Odin James (wait—those initials, O.J., seem familiar somehow . . .) is the only black kid at an exclusive all-white prep school, but he's there because he's a basketball superstar. (Nope, no racial stereotypes there.) Hugo, one of the guys on his team, is insanely jealous because he feels ignored and passed over by the coach, who (in one of the movie's nicer additions) *is also his father*. As Iago does in the play, Hugo sets wheels in motion to take his revenge, using and manipulating Odin's loving and intense relationship with Desi, the dean's daughter.

So far, so straightforward. The problem is, without Shakespeare's poetry, the movie is only about watching the pieces of a tragic jigsaw puzzle fall into place. It most comes to life when writer/director Nelson finds a modern equivalent for Shakespeare's heightened text: rap music on the soundtrack, the inspirational speeches by the coach, the flirtatious banter by the two lovers, and the hip-hop slanguage used by pretty much everybody.

The basketball scenes are exciting, demonstrating visually why Odin is so gifted and why his fall is so dramatic, and high school is the perfect setting for portraying stupid and immature romantic jealousies. Odin's ability to accept Hugo's lies about Desi's infidelity is pretty hard to buy, but we're forced to accept it as his "tragic flaw." Sigh. Tragic flaws are tough to play. Mekhi Phifer gives it his all: He's endearingly in love at the beginning, and as he grows suspicious about Desi, he becomes convincingly tortured about what he has to do. It's only in the actual moments of transition you don't buy it (or maybe you only buy it if you're a teen still tortured by romantic betrayal, or fantasies of romantic betrayal).

This is a good intro to *Othello* if the idea of watching actual Shakespeare sounds too intimidating (which would be silly because the Laurence Fishburne version is pretty neophyte-friendly). And one small reward is that Hugo in this version is actually caught and punished for his actions. We'll take what we can get.

A DOUBLE LIFE (1947)

Directed by George Cukor
Written by Ruth Gordon and Garson Kanin
Rating: 💀💀

A Shakespearean actor's offstage behavior starts to resemble that of his characters, which becomes a problem when his latest role is Othello. Ronald Colman won the Best Actor Oscar playing an actor with a huge identity crisis. The use of Shakespeare's text to underscore his growing madness ("farewell the tranquil mind" echoes repeatedly) is well done, but if you've seen any ventriloquist-who-goes-insane-with-his-murderous-puppet movie, you know where this one's going.

The biggest problem, of course, is that nowadays a plot about an actor who turns into the parts he plays sounds like the premise of a Rob Schneider movie, not the stuff of dramatic tragedy.

PERICLES
FilmVersions: One
Notable Film Versions: Nope.

This baby is due for an epic film treatment: it's got romance, storms at sea, pirates, everything a successful Hollywood blockbuster needs . . .well, except for a recognizable title and a compelling storyline. Never mind.

RICHARD II
FilmVersions: Eight
Notable Film Versions: One

The standout here is the BBC version (1978) starring Derek Jacobi. Jacobi's always good.
Rating: 💀💀

RICHARD III
Film Versions: Eight
Notable Film Versions: Two

Richard III (1955)
Directed by Laurence Olivier
Cedric Hardwicke as King Edward IV of England
Laurence Olivier as Richard III
Ralph Richardson as Duke of Buckingham
John Gielgud as George, Duke of Clarence
Claire Bloom as Lady Anne
Rating: 💀💀💀💀

Richard III (1995)

Directed by Richard Loncraine
Ian McKellen as Richard III
Annette Bening as Queen Elizabeth
Jim Broadbent as Duke of Buckingham
Robert Downey Jr. as Anthony, Earl of Rivers
Nigel Hawthorne as George, Duke of Clarence
Kristin Scott Thomas as Lady Anne
John Wood as King Edward IV
Maggie Smith as Duchess of York

Rating: 💀💀💀💀💀

Richard III is all about killing, which makes it a natural for the movies. Olivier's version is the "classic" version, with original period costumes, almost the whole text (*oy . . .*), and Olivier working at the absolute top of his game both in front of the camera and behind. McKellen's version is the definitive "interpretive" version, conceived in nonpurist terms as a contemporary movie, with a newly conceived setting and much of the text cut or reordered.[84]

The story, in the simplest of terms, is that Richard III wants to become king of England and will do anything to achieve his goal. This mainly involves murdering all his friends and relatives, which leads to civil war.

This is where the McKellen version gets confusing. The film is set in the 1930s, when England was not, in fact, embroiled in a civil war. Obviously, this is simply a "directorial conceit," mixing fantasy with fact, like an Oliver Stone movie, only classier.

The soldiers are dressed in beige and black uniforms, which gives the movie a cool neo-fascist look, further intensified by location shooting at the Battersea Power Station in South London, a building that also appears on the cover of Pink Floyd's *Animals* album, which is similarly Orwellian, though not Shakespearean.

---

[84] For everything you ever wanted to know about Olivier's *Richard III,* we recommend Russell Lees's audio commentary on the Criterion Collection DVD. It's informed as much by his knowledge of the play as by his experience as a playwright and director. True, he's a friend of ours, but he's still pretty knowledgeable. A little too knowledgeable, if you ask us.

This confusion might be alleviated if you could watch the first two movies in the trilogy, but *Richard II* is hard to find and Shakespeare never wrote anything called *Richard I*.[85]

Nevertheless, the cast in the McKellen version is full of excellent British actors whom you may recognize from their work on little-watched PBS programs. Ian McKellen is brilliant in the title role. He's a marvelous villain; plotting, scheming, wenching, and murdering with undisguised glee. His performance carefully incorporates characteristics of several real-life right-wingers: the mustache of Hitler, the jelly beans of Ronald Reagan, the withered arm of Bob Dole. And he plays the film's comic highlight (in which Richard quotes Catherine the Great: "A horse, a horse! My kingdom for a horse!") with just the right amount of what-the-hell-am-I-doing-here frustration.

Apparently, Annette Bening and Robert Downey Jr. were cast because the producers wanted two huge American movie stars, but unfortunately couldn't find any. Bening and Junior show the Brits how to perform Shakespeare in the finest Reduced Shakespeare Company tradition: They're shrill, nasal, over-the-top, and completely superficial. God bless America.

Movies Based on RICHARD III

LOOKING FOR RICHARD (1996)

This is Al Pacino's documentary about putting on his stage production of *Richard III*. For some theater folk, it's an absorbing look at the creative process. For most anyone else, a wanky, self-absorbed journey about how tough an actor's life is. Please.

Rating: Zero Bards

ROMEO AND JULIET
Film Versions: Forty
Notable Film Versions: Three
Like the film versions of *Hamlet*, every generation gets its own *Romeo and Juliet*.

---

[85] This is another reason why Hollywood is so hot on Shakespeare: The Bard loved sequels.

Romeo and Juliet (1936)
Directed by George Cukor
Norma Shearer as Juliet
Leslie Howard as Romeo
John Barrymore as Mercutio
Basil Rathbone as Tybalt
Rating: 💀💀.

Romeo and Juliet (1968)
Directed by Franco Zeffirelli
Leonard Whiting as Romeo
Olivia Hussey as Juliet
John McEnery as Mercutio
Milo O'Shea as Friar Laurence
Michael York as Tybalt
Rating: 💀💀

William Shakespeare's Romeo + Juliet (1996)
Directed by Baz Luhrmann
Written by Craig Pearce and Baz Luhrmann
Leonardo DiCaprio as Romeo
Claire Danes as Juliet
John Leguizamo as Tybalt
Paul Sorvino as Fulgencio Capulet
Brian Dennehy as Ted Montague
Pete Postlethwaite as Friar Laurence
Rating: 💀💀💀💀💀

The movie and casting couldn't be more wrong and dated in George Cukor's 1936 version, but it's strangely compelling.

Teenage Romeo and Juliet are played by the forty-three-year-old pre–*Gone With the Wind* Leslie Howard, and thirty-four-year-old Norma Shearer, who's filmed through about seventeen layers of Vaseline. There's lots of additional expository dialogue that's not remotely Shakespearean, and the clashing of metal swords in the opening street battle sounds like the clatter of actual wood. The leads, while completely miscast, sure do understand the language (although Shearer sings it and flits around the gardens and her bedchamber with her hands atwitter in a ghastly illusion of youth). John Barrymore (Drew's grandfather) plays the hot-blooded teen Mercutio, but at age fifty-four is way too old and works way too hard.

Cukor directs the first half of the movie as if it were a screwball comedy—Andy Devine and Edna May Oliver are particularly broad—but once Mercutio's killed, there's a major tonal shift and it becomes Shakespeare's classic tragedy.[86]

Franco Zeffirelli mostly abandons the comedy in his 1968 version, focusing instead on the intense passion of youth. He cast (gasp!) *actual teens* in the title roles, and they're *adorable!* Who cares if Juliet sounds like she's dubbed by about four different actresses? Who cares if Romeo doesn't really seem like he understands what he's saying (and is so sexless that Zeffirelli had to cut his line, "My love has made me effeminate!")? They were the perfect symbols of the 1960s youth culture, and the honesty of their emotions gives their tragedy a truer poignancy than the great acting but wildly inappropriate ages of the 1936 version. Incredibly successful on its first release, people's fondness for it seems inversely related to how old they were when they first saw it.

Baz Luhrmann's *William Shakespeare's Romeo + Juliet*, on the other hand, is tragedy from the get-go (inspired by Shakespeare's prologue, which, as we pointed out previously, totally gives the game away). Violence is everywhere in the Miami-like "Verona Beach"; it's a way of life, and the love these two teens share is an all-too-brief escape before they meet their tragic ends.

However, as tragedies go, this one is spectacularly up-tempo and high-energy. Luhrman uses jump cuts, a brilliantly percusive contemporary soundtrack, and incredibly detailed production design to bring clarity to the various rivalries and allegiances and greater understanding to the text.

And the cast is terrific. Leonardo DiCaprio is the hottest

---

[86] Director Jonathan Demme and screenwriter E. Max Frye brilliantly re-created this shift in tone in *Something Wild* (1986), starring Melanie Griffith, Jeff Daniels, and Ray Liotta. It starts off as a screwball comedy, then becomes a different kind of movie entirely. If you must choose between the 1936 *Romeo and Juliet* or *Something Wild*, we suggest *Something Wild*.

Romeo on record, the physical embodiment of everything a teenage girl would kill herself for (or so we're told). Claire Danes is lovely and genuinely appealing, and also "displays that elusive 'wiser-than-her-years' quality that the part demands."[87] Harold Perrineau (of TV's *Lost*) is a madly flamboyant Mercutio; John Leguizamo, an oily Flamenco gunfighter Tybalt; Pete Postlethwaite, a Goth priest; M. Emmet Walsh, the scuzzball Apothecary; and Brian Dennehy and Paul Sorvino the doomed lovers' fathers. Each role is freshly conceived in this modern adaptation.

Baz Luhrmann is known (and sometimes criticized) for his wildly elaborate designs and frantic editing. But it's his skill with actors and his attention to even the smallest of behavioral details that make his movies compelling. His choice to have Juliet wake up just before Romeo kills himself is inspired and makes you wonder why it's not always done like that. She's too groggy to say anything and he's too busy soliloquizing to notice she's awake, and the tragedy (which looks for once like it might be avoided) is only intensified.

Movies Based on *ROMEO AND JULIET*

WEST SIDE STORY (1961)
Directed by Jerome Robbins
Based on the musical by Arthur Laurents (book), Stephen Sondheim (lyrics), and Leonard Bernstein (music)
Rating:
This is the classic reimagining of the Houses of Montague and Capulet as rival New York City street gangs. The dancing tough guys convey just as much macho menace as the original play's guys-in-tights biting their thumbs at one another. Unfortunately.

THE TAMING OF THE SHREW
Film Versions: Fourteen
Notable Film Versions: Three

---

[87] According to Daniel Rosenthal in *Shakespeare on Screen*, p. 131.

The Taming of the Shrew (1929)
Directed by Sam Taylor
Mary Pickford as Katharine
Douglas Fairbanks as Petruchio
Rating: 💀💀💀

One of the very first "talkie" Shakespeare films, it's surprisingly wonderful. Mary Pickford is maybe a little out of her element, but Fairbanks brings both vitality and sexuality to his role. The advertising tagline was "All Talking! All Laughing!" and, clocking in at sixty-six minutes, it was also "All over in little over an hour!"

The Taming of the Shrew (1967)
Directed by Franco Zeffirelli
Elizabeth Taylor as Katharine
Richard Burton as Petruchio
Rating: 💀💀💀

When introducing this version to his University of California at Berkeley "Shakespeare on Film" course, Professor Hugh Richmond gave an artistic assessment of the film that really made us horny college students sit up and take notice. He said, "Miss Taylor's décolletage makes up for any *serious* acting deficiency," and by God, he wasn't kidding. "Violet eyes to die for" be damned; she's got many other magnificent parts to die for as well. But give the diva her due: She's really pretty good as the violent, tantrum-throwing troublesome wench. And her performance as Kate isn't bad either.

She's joined onscreen by her on-again, off-again husband/lover Richard Burton, whose legendary love of liquor fuels this performance, as well. Rowdy, robust, over the top: this Petruchio and Kate totally deserve each other, and yet Zeffirelli's direction allows for quiet moments when the camera lingers on Liz (*purr*) and Dick (*rowr*) and you see the quiet desperation of two characters who might actually be genuinely in love with each other.

This film was critically maligned on its release, but we maintain that it's unjustly underrated. It does what a Shakespeare movie should do: It gets past the language, making cuts if necessary, and gets to the character. No less an authority than Jeremy Irons says (in an interview we can't find anymore, so we can't cite it exactly) that much of Shakespeare's language is spent setting up the scene, describing the place and the weather. On stage (and in the woefully underfunded BBC versions), all you *have* is the language, but on film, you can show those things, freeing up the language to focus on character and story. Linger on the language at your peril—get to the characters. Tell the story. Zeffirelli does this brilliantly. We often speak of the great Shakespearean filmmakers Olivier, Branagh, and even Orson Welles, but Zeffirelli's film adaptations are probably the most in the spirit of the original Elizabethan stage productions: They're hugely energetic, popular, critics-be-damned crowd-pleasers of which, we feel, Shakespeare himself would have heartily approved.

The Taming of the Shrew (1980)
Directed by Jonathan Miller
John Cleese as Petruchio
Sarah Badel as Catarina/Kate
Rating: Zero Bards

We include this version because it's notably *bad* and you'll be tempted to rent it because of its pedigree. Don't. This has to be listed under the heading of Big Disappointments. You'd think that if you were going to get a bunch of people together and spend some money to film a Shakespeare play for posterity, you should at least have some general idea about how that might be done. The BBC apparently thought casting John Cleese as Petruchio was the only idea they needed to have. It wasn't.

Cleese is a very smart Petruchio, very controlled, and can't help but be very funny in spots, but he seems to be playing the role as a kind of academic exercise without in any sense giving a performance, no doubt encouraged by his director, the dryly cerebral *Beyond the Fringe* veteran Jonathan Miller. Cleese simply isn't very fun, which in a comedy is kind of a drag. His Petruchio doesn't change so much as reveal himself over the course of the play. Sarah Badel is a petulant Kate: more effective in her quiet moments, but not in any sense suggesting the shrewish extremes in the characters that keep Padua so on edge.

You keep wishing there were a strong point of view, or at least an interesting one. It seems that Miller's only goal was to shoot everything in one take, in the style of a live television drama from the 1950s. Director and cast never find any varying levels, and it's all boringly domestic, like a sedate and uninteresting dinner party—which is exactly how Miller stages the final scene. This is then followed by the cast singing a contrapuntal Elizabethan ditty *a capella*; really, it couldn't be more quaint and sleep-inducing.

True aficionados of dry humor will not be disappointed, however. Also included in the cast is the guy who played Mr. Peacock in the classic BBC sitcom *Are You Being Served?* BBC in this case stands for Bad British Comedy.

ESSAY QUESTION: *Have you seen John Cleese's crowning achievements* Fawlty Towers *and* A Fish Called Wanda? *If not, get thee hence to your nearest online video establishment and watch the man in his absolute glory. If you're not familiar with Cleese's other work (a group of fellows known collectively as Monty Python's Flying Circus), you're beyond redemption.*

Movies Based on TAMING OF THE SHREW

10 THINGS I HATE ABOUT YOU (1999)
Directed by Gil Junger
Written by Karen McCullah Lutz and Kirsten Smith
Heath Ledger as Patrick "Pat" Verona
Julia Stiles as Katarina "Kat" Stratford
Rating: 💀 💀 💀 💀

A surprisingly likable version of *Shrew* set in a turn-of the-twentieth-century high school.[88] It begins as an ominously crass

---

[88] Can you say *fin de siècle* if it refers to the end of the *twentieth* century? Or is that too wanky?

teen sex comedy, with gratuitous references to male genitalia that promise more dirt than the movie (fortunately) delivers. But by the end, it becomes a warm and, if still not terribly mature, at least sincere romantic comedy.

As in all romantic comedies, the form requires the main lovers to hate each other at the beginning but fall for each other at the end. The trick is keeping the lovers apart for an hour and a half. These rituals are properly observed, and it's shocking to realize, seeing how easily Shakespeare works in modern settings, the extent to which contemporary romantic comedies (and television sitcoms) are almost religiously formulaic, and how Shakespeare himself invented, or at least perfected, the formulas.[89]

There's very little of the text of Shakespeare's *Shrew* in the screenplay, but Shakespeare himself—his face, his words, his spirit —informs many of the movie's touches. The setting is Padua High School (filmed in a real Tacoma, Washington, school that looks like an Elizabethan castle), and one of the tertiary lovers woos his potential girlfriend with Shakespearean verse. Several of the actors (Julia Stiles and Andrew Keegan, primarily) have made minicareers acting in filmed updates of Shakespeare, notably *O*, *Hamlet* (Stiles played Ophelia opposite Ethan Hawke), and *A Midsummer Night's Rave*. The soundtrack features pop songs that underscore Shakespeare's romantic themes, especially "I Want You to Want Me" and the particularly *Shrew*-specific "Cruel to Be Kind."

After Padua High's English teacher performs part of Sonnet 141 as a hip-hop rap, he says, "I know Shakespeare's a dead white guy, but he knows his shit." Yes, he does, my friend. Yes, he does.

KISS ME KATE (1953)
Directed by George Sidney
Based on the musical by Cole Porter (songs) and Sam and Bella Spewack (script)

---

[89] Go ahead, ask yourself: How many sitcom plots have hinged on people betting they can date a beautiful woman or paying someone else to do so?

Kathryn Grayson as Lilli Vanessi ("Katharine")
Howard Keel as Fred Graham ("Petruchio")
Ann Miller as Lois Lane ("Bianca")
Keenan Wynn as Lippy
James Whitmore as Slug
Rating: 💀 💀 💀 💀

This is Cole Porter's famous play-within-a-musical version, featuring a bickering and once-married pair of theatrical divas who are persuaded to star together again in a musical version of *Taming of the Shrew*, and play characters only slightly less obnoxious than they are. Porter takes many of his musical cues directly from Shakespeare's text (Petruchio's "I've Come to Wive It Wealthily in Padua," and "Where Is the Life That Late I Led?"; Kate's "I Am Ashamed That Women Are So Simple," and the show's title), and serves up one of history's greatest tributes to the Bard in the pun-filled "Brush Up Your Shakespeare."

THE TEMPEST
Film Versions: Fourteen
Notable Film Versions: None

Shakespeare's last great play has defeated the many filmmakers who've attempted to turn it into a movie. The problem seems to be the balancing of tones, as no one seems able to manage the combination of romance, drama, reality, and magic.

Derek Jarman's experimental 1979 version was filmed on location in an ancient English abbey, where he created the wild island of the play mostly indoors. Wonderful imagery meets terrible acting, at times completely unwatchable, and yet you can't take your eyes away. The result is a viewing experience that feels like you've stumbled into a party to which you haven't been invited.

Rating: 💀 💀 💀

Movies Based on THE TEMPEST

FORBIDDEN PLANET (1956)

Awww . . . watching this is like playing with an old plastic toy you loved as a child: It's cute, but doesn't deliver the same thrills it once did. Its reputation as a sci-fi version of *The Tempest* is misleading (it's based as much on *Dr. Jekyll and Mr. Hyde* as it is Shakespeare's play), but it's a quaint combination of 1930s radio drama (it's so talky!), 1940s Freudian fascination, 1950s intellectual paranoia, and special effects that are pure state-of-the-artifice.

Rating:

PROSPERO'S BOOKS (1991)
Directed by Peter Greenaway
Sir John Gielgud as Prospero

This is a movement-based, living-breathing-and-dancing painting-come-to-life with Prospero (Gielgud in one of his final film roles) reciting all the lines from *The Tempest* himself. Lots of folks love it, including one or two people whose opinions we respect. But for us, Greenaway's refusal to tell the story and his criminal waste of Gielgud in what could have been a defining late-career role is unforgivable. Shore is purty, though.

Rating:

TIMON OF ATHENS
Film Versions: One
Notable Film Versions: One
Directed by Jonathan Miller (1981)
Jonathan Pryce as Timon

Miller just might make up for his *Shrew* here . . . but we don't know 'cause we haven't seen it.[90]

TITUS ANDRONICUS
Film Versions: Four
Notable Film Versions: One

---

[90] Why? Because it's *Timon of Athens,* people! And we already feel burned by Miller's *Shrew*. Fool us once, shame on you. Fool us twice, shame on us.

Titus (1999)
Written and directed by Julie Taymor
Anthony Hopkins as Titus
Jessica Lange as Tamora
Rating: 💀💀

After her success directing the Broadway production of *The Lion King*, Julie Taymor directed this definitive film version of *Titus Andronicus*, and got to work with Oscar-winning puppets, too. The main pleasure here is watching Anthony Hopkins tear into a Shakespearean role with a relish worthy of Hannibal Lecter; this could be his *Silence of the Iambs*. The other pleasure here is all the blood: If your parents are after you to quit renting those stupid teenage splatter movies and watch something cultural instead, then this blood's for you. (Check out *Theater of Blood* and Polanski's *Macbeth*, too.)

TROILUS AND CRESSIDA
Film Versions: Three
Notable Film Versions: None

TWELFTH NIGHT
Film Versions: Fifteen
Notable Film Versions: Two

Twelfth Night (1996)
Directed by Trevor Nunn
Helena Bonham Carter as Olivia
Nigel Hawthorne as Malvolio
Ben Kingsley as Feste
Mel Smith as Sir Toby Belch
Imelda Staunton as Maria
Richard E. Grant as Sir Andrew Aguecheek
Rating: 💀💀💀

It's a shame that Trevor Nunn never gets the big budgets some of his other fellow Shakespeare filmers get. His ability to underscore and illustrate a play's back story, and justify theatrical devices that work better onstage than on the screen is (with the possible exception of Kenneth Branagh) unmatched.

Case in point: *Twelfth Night*. Nunn opens the film with a lively party and an entertainment at sea that is tragically interrupted by a shockingly realistic storm. This establishes two things: The narrow escape Viola makes as her beloved brother is drowned (or so she thinks); and the fact that Viola has experience dressing in disguise. It also adds a psychological component: Though she dresses as a man to hide herself in an enemy land, she impersonates her *brother* to keep his image alive.

It also allows Nunn to add some funny physical business as Viola is forced to carry her impersonation to its logical ends: smoking, playing pool, and riding horses with Duke Orsino, on whom she has her unrevealable crush. Unfortunately, Nunn isn't able to sustain this comic tone throughout the movie, which is surprisingly wistful and bittersweet. Ben Kingsley brings great depth and subtle wit, but not much life, to the role of Feste. Mel Smith (the Albino from *The Princess Bride*) and Richard E. Grant (*Withnail & I*) bring more energy to the proceedings, but the object of their revenge, Malvolio (at least as embodied by Nigel Hawthorne), seems more tortured than teased. Or maybe we don't find torture as funny as we used to.

However, Nunn is brilliant at getting actors to throw away Shakespearean affectation and treat the dialogue as simple conversation. The scenes between Kingsley and Imelda Staunton (*Vera Drake*) crackle with ease and intelligence. It's a lesson Sir Peter Hall never learned (or, in his defense, simply isn't interested in), and many other directors can't even approach.

Twelfth Night (2003)
Directed by Tim Supple
Parminder Nagra as Viola
Chiwetel Ejiofor as Orsino
Rating: 🎭🎭
Tim Supple's version uses multi-ethnic casting that illustrates quite well the differences in culture and class that were

more apparent to Shakespeare's original audience. Although it's more interesting as a theatrical exercise than an actual movie, not as funny as the actors playing Toby Belch and Sir Andrew think it is, and hard to understand if you don't know the play well, the lead performance from *ER*'s Parminder Nagra (the girl from *Bend It Like Beckham*) is very strong and appealing.

Two Gentlemen of Verona
Film Versions: One
Notable Film Versions: None

The Winter's Tale
Film Versions: Five
Notable Film Versions: None

Movies Based on Shakespeare's Work, Life, and Influence

Shakespeare: The Animated Tales (1992)
Adapted by Leon Garfield
Rating: 💀💀💀💀

Twelve of Shakespeare's most popular works, each beautifully animated in its own unique style, featuring the voices of Hugh Grant and several dozen members of the Royal Shakespeare Company. Each tale is only twenty-five minutes long, so it's terrific for kids or anyone with a short attention span (which is probably why we like it so much).

Shakespeare in Love (1998)
Directed by John Madden
Written by Marc Norman and Tom Stoppard
Joseph Fiennes as William Shakespeare
Gwyneth Paltrow as Viola
Geoffrey Rush as Philip Henslowe
Colin Firth as Lord Wessex
Judi Dench as Queen Elizabeth
Rating: 💀💀💀💀💀

A wonderful romantic comedy that just happens to star the greatest playwright in the history of the world. The depiction of Shakespeare as young, horny, and struggling for ideas is a funny place to start, and the movie just gets better as it satirizes show business and imagines how love transformed both Shakespeare and his work. With true and funny insights into the creative process and the bonds that are forged when putting on a show, it's an irreverent and funny celebration of Shakespeare the poet, backstage romance, young love, and artistic inspiration.

THEATER OF BLOOD (1973)

Vincent Price as a famous Shakespearean actor who takes revenge on his critics, killing each of them in high style, using methods inspired by Shakespeare's plays. Bloody good fun.

Rating: 🎭🎭🎭🎭

Fig. 21. The inscription on Shakespeare's burial place at Stratford-upon-Avon. Hey, folks! How about fixing the cracks? For goodness sake, he was the greatest playwright in history!

CONCLUSION

"We'll see thee anon. And on, and on, and on . . ."
—*Anythynge You Want To: Shakespeare's Lost Comedie,*
Firesign Theater

nd there you have it.
Shakespeare's life, plays,
poems, movies, and legacy
summarily dealt with. How'd we do?

More important, how'd *you* do? Let's see how well you answered the questions we asked in our Introduction:

1. **What is believed to be the first play that Shakespeare wrote?**
   Two Gentlemen of Verona, in 1590–1.
2. **What is believed to be the last play he wrote?**
   Two Noble Kinsmen, co-written with John Fletcher in 1613–4.
3. **Which two books did Shakespeare use as general references for his history plays?**
   The Chronicles of England, Ireland, and Scotland by Raphael Holinshed and *The Union of the Two Noble and Illustre Families of Lancaster and York* by Edward Hall.
4. **Name the four major poems attributed to Shakespeare, other than the sonnets.**
   "A Lover's Complaint," "Venus and Adonis," "The Rape of Lucrece," and "The Phoenix and the Turtle."
5. **Which two monarchs ruled England during Shakespeare's lifetime?**
   Elizabeth I and James I.

6. **What is the First Folio? Name the two people most responsible for its publication.**

   It is the first published collection of Shakespeare's plays. The two people responsible for its publication were John Hemminges and Henry Condell. We will also accept the answer William Jaggard (who printed it) or Edward Blount (who went bankrupt publishing it) and be damned impressed that you came up with it.

7. **What is a Quarto?**

   A printed version of a single play.

8. **Name four London theaters in which Shakespeare's plays may have been first performed.**

   The Theater, the Rose, the Blackfriars, and the Globe.

9. **How many plays are generally attributed to Shakespeare?**

   Thirty-nine.

10. **How many sonnets are attributed to him?**

    One hundred fifty-four.

11. **How many children did Shakespeare have?**

    Three: Susanna (b. 1583) and twins, Hamnet and Judith (b. 1585)

12. **How many brothers and sisters did Shakespeare have?**

    He was the third of eight children.

13. **What were the names of Shakespeare's parents?**

    John and Mary (Arden) Shakespeare.

14. **What was the name of Shakespeare's dog?**

    Spot. He's mentioned in *Macbeth*: "Out, out, damned Spot!"

15. **What was the name of his wife?**

    Trick question: Spot didn't have a wife. Shakespeare, however, was married to Anne (Hathaway) Shakespeare.

16. **Where was Shakespeare both born and buried?**

    Stratford-upon-Avon, Warwickshire, England.

17. **Which two actors were *not* members of Shakespeare's acting company: Richard Burbage, Henry Condell, John Hemminges, Harry Dean Stanton, William Kempe, Robert Armin, Thomas Pope, Augustine Phillips, or Jerry Mathers?**

    Another trick question. There are, in fact, millions of actors who were not members of Shakespeare's acting company.

18. **Who is believed to be the "Dark Lady" of the sonnets?**

    Gwyneth Paltrow. (Seriously, there's no other best guess these days. Unless you think the Dark Lady was Whoopi Goldberg, in which case we salute your irreverence.)

19. **What type of verse did Shakespeare use most commonly in his plays?**

    Iambic pentameter. Iambic refers to one stressed syllable followed by an unstressed syllable. Pentameter means there are five stressed syllables per line.

20. **Which of Shakespeare's plays was likely the most popular during his lifetime?**

    Titus Andronicus, believe it or not.

Check your scoring. If you got:

15–20 correct answers, you're a true Shakespeare geek, more to be pitied than admired.

10–15 correct answers, not bad but still far from ideal—you probably still live with your parents.

5–10 correct answers, you're about average—there's a chance you could get a date if you really tried.

Fewer than five correct answers, congratulations! You've enjoyed this book without paying too much attention. You might also still have a life!

But is that it? Does any of this knowledge and analysis begin to explain our fascination with a four-hundred-year-old playwright? What is it about a guy who wrote plays that most of us find intimidating in a language most of us don't understand? It's very simple.

Shakespeare is *we*.

Or, to put it another way, Shakespeare are us.

The very fact that we know so little about him is what draws us to him. Shakespeare is the Chauncey Gardner of literature, a blank slate on which we create the image of the playwright as we want him to be.[91] Like a Rorschach test, our conjectures reveal

---

[91] Chauncey Gardner is the character played by Peter Sellers in the movie *Being There*, which is based on the novel by Jerzy Kosinski. This means, unfortunately, that *Chauncey Gardner* is the Chauncey Gardner of literature. But you get the idea.

more about ourselves than they do about Shakespeare. We want Shakespeare to have risen from humble middle-class origins because so many of us have done so. We resist the notion that Shakespeare was a genius because most of us aren't. We celebrate the fact that Shakespeare wrote, acted, abandoned his family, and slept around indiscriminately because that's what we've . . . never mind. The point is, other people see him differently:

- When screenwriter Marc Norman says "Shakespeare would have had a three-picture deal at Warner Brothers, driven a Porsche, and had a house in Bel-Air," it's because that's what Marc Norman wants (or has).
- When George Bernard Shaw says he wants to dig up Shakespeare's corpse and throw stones at it, he displays an astonishing degree of self-loathing.
- When scholars call Shakespeare their "gravy train," it's because they've eaten dog food.
- When we call Shakespeare a savvy, irreverent, poetic, literary, sartorial, marketing, financial, romantic, myth-making, entertainment genius . . . well, obviously it's because we have our own impossible ambitions.
- And, most important, you, the reader, undoubtedly think of Shakespeare as an intelligent person with a great sense of humor who'd buy a dozen copies of this book to give away as presents.

Shakespeare, as Hamlet says in his advice to the players, is the mirror we hold up to ourselves. Because we know so little about him, Shakespeare becomes the "Shakespeare" we aspire to be, the "Shakespeare" in all of us.

And the more we know about him, the more we know ourselves. Thanks for reading. It seems only fitting to give the Bard the final words . . .

> Have more than thou showest,
> Speak less than thou knowest,
> Lend less than thou owest.
>> *King Lear*, Act I, Scene 4

To thine own self be true.
> *Hamlet*, Act I, Scene 3

And of course,

Sell when you can, you are not for all markets.
> *As You Like It*, Act III, Scene 5

Reed Martin
Austin Tichenor
Sonoma and Los Angeles, California, 2005

Backword

by William Shakespeare

Welcome hither! How you been? Things, for me, are going *great*, thanks for asking. I've been dead almost four hundred years but in the words of that great commercial, my memory lives on in this new collection from K-Tel and in, man, it seems like *millions* of books, like this one, all claiming to know me and my works.

Well, tell the truth and shame the devil (to coin a phrase, something I did more than once), people *don't* know me. Nobody knows me, which is just the way I like it. You think you know me? Here's something I never told anybody: They call me the Bard of Avon, but did you know they also used to call me Will the Thrill, Shakey-Breaky, and (once) Nancy? Of course you didn't. Who would brag about something like that?

And here's another thing you don't know. Since I'm back—and damn, it feels good to be writing again—I want you to be the first to know I'm petitioning Congress to extend the Copyright Law. That's right—extend that bad boy. Right now a copyright lasts only, what, seventy-five years after a writer's death? Screw that. These words are mine! I own them. Hell, in many cases I in-vented them! In fact, I should trademark some of them, and I'll be drafting legislation that says I get a nickel every time you use the word "generous."

The free ride's over, people. I want the money that's owed me. From now on, when you perform one of my plays, I get a piece of the action from dime one. When you make a movie out of one of my plays, I get an executive producer credit and you pay first-class expenses the whole way for me and mine.

Oh, and don't forget Lindsay Lohan. Have that cutie-patootie sent to my trailer, pronto.

Man, it is good to be back. Thanks for having me. Let's get this party started.

William Shakespeare
Cabo San Lucas

P.S. Watch out, I just saw Jesus. He's coming back, too, and he doesn't look happy.

Bibliography

Impossible though it may be to believe, we cracked a book or two before we wrote this baby (and once or twice during it). All of the following were incredibly helpful and several of them were delightful, as well. But be careful: The pool of Shakespearean scholarship is deep and turbulent. Stay with us in the shallow end. No lifeguard on duty. No running. No diving. No peeing.

Disclaimer: One or two of the following titles may look strange or out of place. All we can say is that we would have used them as references if they actually existed.

Asimov, Isaac. *Asimov's Chronology of the World*. New York: HarperCollins, 1991.
Everything that ever happened, going all the way back to the beginning of time. Sadly, the world apparently ended in 1991, so we'll never know how things turned out.

Angelou, Maya. *I Know Why the Caged Bard Sings*. New York, 1983.
Can't keep a good bard down.

Bangs, Lester. *Shakespeare, Rattle, and Roll*. New York, 1971.
"Sigh not so and let them go / Be you blithe and bonnie / Converting all your songs of woe / Into hey nonnie nonnie." *Much Ado About Nothing*, Act II, Scene 3

Bloom, Harold. *Shakespeare—The Invention of the Human*. New York: Riverhead Books, 1998.
Great plays, beautiful sonnets, upright bipeds with opposable thumbs: Shakespeare could invent anything.

Branagh, Kenneth. *Beginning*. New York: St. Martin's Press, 1989.
Still waiting for the sequel, entitled *Middle*.

Brown, Dan. *The Shakespeare Code*. New York, 2003.
Robert Langdon exposes another Vatican conspiracy. This time it's the one where rogue cardinals try to keep the true author of Shakespeare's plays a secret.

Chute, Marchette. *Shakespeare of London*. New York: E. P. Dutton, 1949.
That's what it said on his business cards.

————. *Stories from Shakespeare*. New York: Mentor, 1976.
An Elizabethan traveling salesman ... well, you get the idea.

Dostoyevsky, Fyodor. *The Brothers Shakespeare*. St. Petersburg, 1873.
Shakespeare's descendants moved to Russia.

Doyle, John and Ray Lischner. *Shakespeare For Dummies*. Wiley, 1999.
A great reference work, but not to be confused with this book, which is Shakespeare *by* dummies.

Dunton-Downer, Leslie and Alan Riding. *Essential Shakespeare Handbook*. DK Publishing, Inc, 2004.
Excellent compendium of Shakespeare facts and figures, but the title's misleading: there's nothing in here about his hands.

Epstein, Norrie. *The Friendly Shakespeare*. New York: Penguin, 1994.
Jasper Fforde, author of *The Eyre Affair* and other Thursday Next books, turned us on to this. A great and easy introduction to Shakespeare. If what we read is true, this book is friendlier than he was.

Farman, John. *The Very Bloody History of Britain*. Red Fox, 1992.
Contains all the good bits of history that teachers usually skip.

Fields, Bertram. *Players: The Mysterious Identity of William Shakespeare*. New York: ReganBooks, 2004.
A great resource if you want a just-the-facts approach without a lot of conjecture. (There's still a *little* conjecture, though. It's hard not to. *You* try writing about Shakespeare without conjecturizing!)

Firesign Theatre. *Anythynge You Want To: Shakespeare's Lost Comedie*, 1977.
Recently discovered, both by them and by us. A fascinating look (and sound) at what might have been . . . if Shakespeare had been four lunatic geniuses with a recording studio at his disposal. Weirdly cool.

Garfield, Leon. *Shakespeare Stories* and *Shakespeare Stories II*. New York: Houghton-Mifflin, 1998, 2000.
Pitched at the fifth-grade-and-up reading level, these story versions of Shakespeare's plays are simplified but by no means dumbed-down. Which means, unfortunately, they're still a little over our heads.

Goddard, Harold. *The Meaning of Shakespeare, Volume 1*. New York: Phoenix Books, 1951.
Wait—there's a second volume? How much meaning can there be? It's possible to have too much meaning, you know. Dial it back, dude.

Greenblatt, Stephen. *Will in the World: How Shakespeare Became Shakespeare.*
New York: W. W. Norton & Company, 2004.
Excellent supposition about Shakespeare's life, but almost nothing about estate planning. Don't be fooled.

Grisham, John. *Runaway Shakespeare.* New York, 1997.
"First thing we do, let's kill all the lawyers." *Henry VI, Part 2,*
Act IV, Scene 2.

Grun, Bernard. *The Timetables of History (The New Third Revised Edition).* New
York: Simon & Schuster, 1963.
1492 x 1776 – 1066 = 1984. Shh. Pass it on.

Hack, Lorenzo. "Shakespeare Is Alive and Living in a Trailer with Elvis." *National Enquirer* (April 7, 1999).
Clearly we're not fussy about our sources.

Harbage, Alfred. *William Shakespeare: A Reader's Guide.* New York: Farrar,
Straus and Giroux, 1963.
Still working on the nonreader's guide.

Hoffman, Calvin. *The Murder of the Man Who Was Shakespeare.* New York:
Grossett & Dunlap, 1955.
Great story. Wouldn't it be neat if it were true?

Ingram, W. G. and Theodore Redpath, eds. *Shakespeare's Sonnets.* Sevenoaks:
Hodder and Stoughton, 1964.
The sonnets are presented here just on their own, with a few notes about
how they should be punctuated. Well, how does that help? How are we supposed to know what to think unless you tell us? From that standpoint, this
book isn't helpful at all.

Jorgens, Jack J. *Shakespeare on Film.* Bloomington: Indiana University Press,
1977.
Captured on a shaky Super-8 camera by a guy on vacation with his family.
Shakespeare can be seen on the left, behind the tree, next to Bigfoot.

Joseph, Bertram. *Acting Shakespeare.* New York: Theater Arts Books, 1969.
Put on a doublet. Grow a beard. Declaim.

Lamb, Charles and Mary. *Tales from Shakespeare.* New York: Puffin Books,
1987.
Sorry—*this* is the nonreader's guide.

Lees, Russell. "DVD Commentary: Laurence Olivier's *Richard III*." Los Angeles: Criterion Edition, 1994.
You really shouldn't know as much about *Richard III* as this guy does. It's not healthy.

Lennon, John and Paul McCartney. *A Bard Day's Night*. London, 1965.
The Fab Four strap on the doublet and hose and quickly discover it's not for them.

Long, Adam, Daniel Singer and Jess Winfield; additional material by Reed Martin. *The Complete Works of William Shakespeare (abridged)*. New York: Applause Books, 1992.
The script that started it all, where Shakespeare saw the possibilities of what his plays could be. Turn to page 124 and wave.

McKellen, Ian. *Richard III: The Annotated Screenplay*. Woodstock: Overlook Press, 1996.
A fascinating look into the process of completely reimagining a great play, and a primer on how to approach Shakespeare with reverent irreverence from a guy with way more credibility than us.

Michell, John. *Who Wrote Shakespeare?* London: Thames & Hudson, 1996.
The guy covers all the bases but inexplicably misses the time-travel angle.

Ney, Charles. "Force of Will." *American Theater*, April 2005.
American Theater publishes articles like this all the time because Shakespeare is America's greatest playwright.

O'Connor, Evangeline M. *Who's Who and What's What in Shakespeare*. London: Avenel Books, 1978.
Not very helpful if you're looking for who's what and when's where.

Onions, C. T., et al. *A Shakespeare Glossary*. London: Oxford University Press, 1986.
This invaluable companion should be at everyone's bedside. You never know when you might have to hurl it at an intruder.

Perry, Anne, ed. *Much Ado About Murder*. New York: Berkley Publishing Group, 2002.
Not helpful, but a lot of fun. A collection of short mysteries based on events from Shakespeare's life and works. Misses the time-travel angle, though.

Rosenthal, Daniel. *Shakespeare on Screen*. London: Hamlyn. 2000.
Handsome and informative coffee-table book, richly illustrated with photos from the movies being discussed. Rosenthal's an excellent critic, but, boy, does he have different tastes than we do. We couldn't disagree more about the John Cleese *Shrew*, for example. Hey, to each his own.

Rowling, J. K. *Harry Potter and the Prisoner of Stratford*. New York, 1999.
Harry leaves Hogwarts and joins the Royal Shakespeare Company, where he gets cast in a production of *Macbeth* directed by He Who Must Not Be Named. Harry, Ron, and Hermione play the weird sisters.

Rowse, A. L. *The Annotated Shakespeare*. London: Greenwich House, 1978.
The ultimate book for footnote fetishists.

Rozakis, Laurie. *The Complete Idiot's Guide to Shakespeare*. New York, Alpha Books, 1999.
Take a right. When you hit London, take a sharp left. When you get to Stratford-upon-Avon, look for the church. Go inside. Underneath the bust of Shakespeare, you'll find the body.
Rubie, Peter. *The Everything Shakespeare Book*. Cincinnati, Adams Media Corporation, 2002.
Turns out the title is a slight overstatement.

Rutherford, Edward. *London*. London: Century Books, 1997.
Not scholarly but fun. A historical novel in the Michener mode. The chapter titled "The Globe" imagines very convincingly the trials, tribulations, and triumphs of the Lord Chamberlain's Men.

Saccio, Peter. *Shakespeare's English Kings*. London: Oxford University Press, 1977.
Turns out that even in those days, royal families were a mess.

Schmidt, Alexander. *Shakespeare Lexicon and Quotation Dictionary, Volumes I & II –Third Edition*. London: Dover, 1971.
Every word defined and located, more than 50,000 quotations identified. Are you man enough? Are you geeky enough? Our question is: Why?

Schoenbaum, Sam. *William Shakespeare: A Documentary Life* and *Shakespeare's Lives*. Oxford: Oxford University Press, 1977, 1991.
These books total more than 900 pages! Based on facts we cover in twelve pages! Color us impressed. *A Documentary Life* is still probably the best biography around, and *Lives* is a fascinating history of Shakespeare biography, how our understanding of the man has grown (or, in our case, shrunk).

Shakespeare, William. *The Complete Works of William Shakespeare*. London: Avenel Books, 1975.
Unabridged!

Smith, Anna Nicole. *Shakespeare's E! True Hollywood Story*. New York, 2002.
Thereby hangs a tale of humble beginnings, early success, descent into drug use and irrelevance, and a phoenixlike rise back to the top. Shakespeare, we mean, not Anna Nicole.

Thomas, Marlo. *Free to Be You and . . .William Shakespeare*. Los Angeles, 2004.
Empowering tale of how you, too, can grow up to be William Shakespeare.

Thomson, Peter. *Shakespeare's Professional Career*. Cambridge: Cambridge University Press, 1992
Fascinating if dry analysis of how Shakespeare made his way in the cutthroat world of Elizabethan theater.

Weir, Alison. *Britain's Royal Families: The Complete Genealogy*. London: Bodley Head, 1989.
Dem kings, dem kings, dem dead kings . . .

Wilson, Jean. *The Archaeology of Shakespeare: The Material Legacy of Shakespeare's Theater*. Cornwall: Alan Sutton Publishing, 1995.
Or, The Globe Theater and What They Found There.

Winfield, Jess. *What Would Shakespeare Do?* Berkeley: Seastone Press, 2000.
We think he'd be flattered by all the attention and buy the first round.

Wood, Michael. *In Search of Shakespeare* (DVD). London: BBC, 2003.
————. *Shakespeare*. New York, Basic Books. 2003.
You know, if our book weren't so bitchin' and wonderful, we'd be giving Wood's DVD and book to both our friends. Very easygoing, and Wood's an engaging host. Still misses the time-travel angle, though. What is it with these people?

Acknowledgments

We'd like to thank our wives, Jane Martin and Dee Ryan, for making all things possible and letting us steal their jokes.

We'd also like to thank a number of people to whom (as far as we know) we're not married:

• Megan Loughney, who dealt with the business details and managed the Reduced Shakespeare Company nerve center so we could focus on the book.

• Our friend Dr. Peter Holland, a genuine Brit and Shakespeare Stud with a wonderful sense of humor, who pointed out all our factual mistakes (any inaccuracies that remain are intended to be in the service of something funny—we hope).

• Playwright, director, and armchair Shakespeare enthusiast Russell Lees, for reading an early manuscript and pretending to laugh, and for not insisting we keep our promise to put his name above the title.

• Christopher Rawson and the *Pittsburgh Post-Gazette* for allowing us to use previously published portions of our reviews of the Laurence Fishburne *Othello* and Ian McKellan *Richard III*.

• Our friends Howard Zimmerman and Roger Cooper at Byron Preiss Visual Publications, for helping us put together the book we wanted to write.

• Kelly Notaras and the gang at Hyperion, for getting it, and selling the heck out of it.

• Michael Faulkner, Joanne Nagel, David Starzyk, George and Melinda Stuart, John Tichenor, and everybody else who loaned us research books, videos, and office space.

• And the late Byron Preiss, who championed us from the beginning and whose idea this all was in the first place. This book wouldn't exist without his faith and support. He will be missed.

Index

Page numbers in *italics* refer to picture captions.

About the Authors

Reed Martin and Austin Tichenor are the owners and Managing Partners of the Reduced Shakespeare Company. They co-created the original stage productions of *The Complete History of America (abridged)*, *The Bible: The Complete Word of God (abridged)*, *Western Civilization: The Complete Musical (abridged)*, *All the Great Books (abridged)*, and *Completely Hollywood (abridged)*, which have been performed all over the world and translated into a dozen languages. They've also written for the BBC, NPR, Britain's Channel Four, RTE Ireland, Public Radio International, the *Washington Post*, the *Pittsburgh Post-Gazette*, and *Vogue* magazine.

Reed's been seen on all the major television networks and has performed in forty-six states and eleven foreign countries, including New Jersey. Prior to joining the Reduced Shakespeare Company, he spent two years as a clown and assistant ringmaster with Ringling Brothers' Barnum & Bailey Circus, where he spent two years frightening children and smelling of elephants. He has a BA in both Theater and Political Science from the University of California at Berkeley and an MFA in Acting from the University of California at San Diego. He is also a graduate of both the Bill Kinnamon School of Professional Umpire Training and Clown College. He lives in northern California with his wife and two sons, and has a strong belief that toilet paper should be fed over the top of the roll.

With Dee Ryan, Austin also wrote and developed the animated project *Fowl Play* for Disney, as well as the screenplays *Birds of a Feather* and *All the Other Reindeer*. He's guest starred on many hours of episodic television, mostly playing impressive Guys in Ties on such shows as *Nip/Tuck*, *24*, *Alias*, *The West Wing*, and *E.R.* He has a BA in History and Dramatic Art from University of California Berkeley and an MFA in Directing from Boston University. He's a member of the Dramatists Guild and an alumnus of the BMI Musical Theater Workshop. He lives in Los Angeles, where he's now hard at work on three screenplays, a novel, and his wife.